Praying for Inner Healing

ROBERT FARICY

*Praying for Inner
Healing*

SCM PRESS LTD

334 01288 0

First published 1979
by SCM Press Ltd
58 Bloomsbury Street London WC1

Second impression 1980

Photoset by John Smith, London
and printed in Great Britain by
Richard Clay (The Chaucer Press) Ltd,
Bungay, Suffolk

# Contents

| | | |
|---|---|---|
| | *Foreword* | vii |
| 1 | Praying to be Healed | 1 |
| 2 | Crying out to the Lord | 17 |
| 3 | By his Wounds we are Healed | 31 |
| 4 | The Cross and Prayer for Inner Healing | 43 |
| 5 | Being Healed through Praise and the Gifts of the Spirit | 56 |
| 6 | Jesus is Lord | 68 |
| | *Notes* | 81 |

# *Foreword*

First, a note to the reader. I wrote this book to help you to pray for your own inner healing. It contains many references to scripture and much theology; I have tried to present food for reflection and for prayer, not at all watered down but set forth in such a way as to be practical. It is a book to be prayed through. 'Out of his infinite glory may he give you the power through his Spirit for your inner self to grow strong' (Eph. 3.16).

I want to thank all who have taught me about praying for inner healing, and particularly Sister Margaret Treacy, Sister Eileen Kennedy, Sister Jean Marie Stross, Diana Villegas Malozemoff, Margaret Schlientz, Fathers Francis MacNutt, Dennis Hamm, Matthew and Dennis Linn, and in a special way Dr Nicolas Camara-Peon.

This book is for Mary and Owen, who prayed with me, and in thanksgiving to the Lord.

# 1

## Praying to be Healed

In recent years, the interest in healing as a response to prayer has grown greatly. Besides the traditional Christian faith in the power of prayer, other factors contribute to this growth of interest: in particular, the charismatic renewal, in which healings of different kinds occur frequently, and the renewal of the sacraments of healing, the sacrament of penance and the sacrament of the anointing of the sick. This chapter outlines briefly the basis, in scripture and in Christian practice, of prayer for healing, and it describes prayer for healing, especially prayer for inner healing.

### Healing in the New Testament

In the gospels, healings take up twenty per cent (in Luke's gospel, one third) of the text. Jesus' ministry is not only to teach, but also to heal; in fact, his self-concept includes, integrally, the idea of being a healer. In the Nazareth synagogue he applies Isaiah 61.1,2 to himself: 'The Spirit of the Lord is upon me, because he has anointed me to preach good news to the poor. He has sent me to proclaim release to the captives and recovering of sight to the blind, to set at liberty those who are oppressed . . .' (Luke 4.18). When John's disciples come to ask him who he is, they find him curing 'many of diseases and plagues and evil spirits', and giving sight to many blind people. He answers them: 'Go

1

and tell John what you have seen and heard: the blind receive their sight, the lame walk, lepers are cleansed, and the deaf hear, the dead are raised up, the poor have good news preached to them' (Luke 7.22).

Jesus' healings are signs of the times, signs of the presence of the Kingdom of God in him. The Kingdom-to-come is already present in the public ministry of Jesus. This is clear from the fact that Jesus acts in the power of the Spirit, the Spirit of the 'last times' when God will pour out his Spirit in the coming of his Kingdom (Joel 2.28-29).

In the past, perhaps, we have not always understood the healings in the gospel in the way that they are presented for our understanding. Jesus' healings have been seen chiefly as demonstrations, even proofs, of his divinity or of his messianic authenticity. In the gospels, however, the 'miracle' aspect, although there, is not accentuated. What is underlined, rather, is that God has come to save us. The saving power of God is present in Jesus to heal us, to save us. The healings that Jesus works are part of, and reveal, the divine work of our salvation.

Not all the gospel cures are physical. Some are spiritual healings: Jesus forgives sins and counsels the sinners to change their lives. And some seem to be psychological healings. Among Jesus' many exorcisms, in which the power of the Spirit of Jesus is contrasted with and seen in opposition to every spirit opposed to God, there appear to be some that are emotional or psychological cures rather than true exorcisms. In the time of the formation of the gospels, mankind had not yet discovered mental illness as a category of human behaviour; it would have been normal to associate psychoses and grave neuroses with the forces of evil, attributing them to unclean or evil spirits. It seems likely that some of the healings that were understood as exorcisms were in reality psychological healings.

2

All Jesus' healings are fruits of his compassion. This compassion, the most obvious quality of his personality and the motivation for his healing ministry, is strongly present in his teaching. He not only forgives sinners – the woman taken in adultery, the paralytic on his mat, Peter, and others – but he also teaches forgiveness. In particular, he preaches the compassion of God for sinners; several parables have the divine compassion as their central point. The God of Jesus' parables is a God who searches out those who need him and his forgiveness: the shepherd searches for the lost sheep; the housewife lights a lamp to look for the lost coin; and the father stands out in the road looking for his son, and finally sees him even while still a long way off. The parable of the prodigal son is not so much about the son as about the prodigal father, prodigal with compassion, forgiveness and goodness. What kind of a person would invent such parables? A person whose own compassion and love was so great that, on his entrance to Jerusalem, ordinary people took off their coats and threw them before him in the street, cut branches off trees and waved them and threw them too in his path and acted so exuberantly as to incur the censure of the leaders of Israel. Jesus is the revelation of the Father; the Father's compassion is mirrored in all Jesus' relationships with others. His table ministry to the prostitutes and tax collectors, especially, shows his compassion; when criticized for his conduct, Jesus replies: 'Those who are well have no need of a doctor, but those who are sick; I came not to call the righteous, but sinners' (Mark 2.17). Breaking bread with sinners is part of his healing ministry; he sees himself as a doctor, a healer.

Jesus' compassionate love has an unrelenting and uncompromising force. Certain parables reflect this 'all-out' aspect of his mercy and love. In the teaching that the Kingdom of Heaven is like a treasure hidden in a field that one buys after selling all other possessions, or like a pearl of great price that a merchant sells all his other pearls to buy, we find Jesus' own attitude towards the Kingdom . He has come to plant the Kingdom in each of us ('the Kingdom of God is within you') so that, in a sense, each of us is the Kingdom for him. That is, each person, for Jesus, is the treasure hidden in the field that, giving up everything else, he buys. And each of us is the pearl of great price; 'you have been ransomed . . . with the precious blood of Christ' (I Peter 1.18-19).

Jesus' disciples continue his ministry of healing (Luke 9.1-2; 9.11; 10.8-9). Jesus is, we might say, 'multiplied' in his disciples; his healing power works through them. In the Acts of the Apostles healing is an integral part of the church's ordinary ministry. In Jesus' name, Peter heals the man lame from birth at the gate called Beautiful (Acts 3.6-7), and Paul heals the cripple at Lystra (Acts 14.10). People place the sick so that at least Peter's shadow can fall on them (Acts 5.15), and handkerchiefs and aprons that Paul touched are brought to the sick – who are healed. Crowds come to Peter for healing (Acts 5.16), just as the Maltese are healed when they come to Paul. A wide variety of ills are healed, ranging from dysentery (Acts 28.8) to complete paralysis (Acts 9.34) and even death (Acts 9.40; 20.10). Healings come about also through Stephen, Philip and Ananias of Damascus; but Peter and Paul are the most important. They stand for the church as a whole, and teach us that Jesus heals in and through his church.

## Christian healing today[1]

According to the promises of Christ (Mark 16.17-18; John 14.12), healings in response to prayer continue; today, they happen with extraordinary frequency, and they constitute certainly a sign of our times. Christian tradition, of course, has always included healings due to God's compassionate intervention. Down through the centuries saints have worked miraculous cures, and praying with faith for the sick has always been part of Christianity. And there have always been shrines at which miraculous cures take place, like Lourdes, Fatima and Guadalupe. Today, however, due to the charismatic renewal and to the renewal of the sacraments of healing, the healing power of the Spirit stands out perhaps more than at any time since early Christianity.

The sacrament of penance is the sacrament of spiritual healing. Spiritual healing consists in receiving God's forgiveness and, at the same time, his power to live in a more Christian way. This double grace, to be forgiven and to do better, is a healing of the soul. Sometimes, in the sacrament of penance, grace overflows and touches in a healing way not only the spiritual but the psychological roots of sinful tendencies; in such cases we can speak of psychological healing. Most confessors have experienced this kind of healing in penitents, healing at both the spiritual and the emotional levels. The renewal of this sacrament has stressed these healing aspects.

The renewal of the sacrament of the anointing of the sick, too, has stressed the sacrament's healing power. This renewal has reoriented the purpose of the sacrament from merely a preparation for death to the complete healing, spiritual and psychological and physical, of all who are seriously sick. This is in keeping with the practice of the early church according to the Letter of James. In fact, the important text of James' letter is read early in the liturgy of the sacrament of the sick:

Is any among you sick? Let him call for the elders of the church, and let them pray over him, anointing him with

5

oil in the name of the Lord; and the prayer of faith will save the sick man, and the Lord will raise him up; and if he has committed sins, he will be forgiven (James 5.14-15).

The eucharist, too, must be considered as a sacrament of healing. After the Second Vatican Council, the renewal of the mass resulted in a clearer understanding of the sacramental grace of the eucharist: the formation of Christian community. This idea, traditional but rediscovered, includes the notion of the healing of interpersonal relationships. 'Because there is one bread, we who are many are one body, for we all partake of the one bread' (I Cor. 10.17); we are one body of Christ because we each receive the one body of Christ. The eucharist is, at the same time, a sacrament of the healing of the individual person. This is why, before communion, the priest prays that the communion be 'a remedy and a defence of both body and soul', and why the congregation prays together, 'say but the word and I shall be healed'.

The charismatic renewal, which has its beginnings in the beginning of Pentecostalism at the turn of the century, entered the mainline Protestant churches and the Roman Catholic church in the 1960s. This renewal has been a shower of graces and gifts and, particularly, of charisms. A charism is a special gift, given not to all but only to some, for the building up of the community; there are many charisms, including teaching, counselling, evangelizing, leading, prophecy, miracles and healing. The new outpouring of charisms of healing, sometimes on individuals and sometimes on groups, has resulted in large numbers of healings of many kinds.

## Inner healing

The most important kind of healing is spiritual healing. In fact, experience shows that physical and psychological healings received as an answer to prayer invariably include, and as a predominant element, a deeper conversion of heart, a new adhesion to the Lord – that is, a spiritual healing. Of course, the physical, the psychological and the spiritual overlap, touch and influence one another; in practice, they can be distinguished but not separated. Spiritual healing will have a psychological component, and psychological healing will often have a physical component in the form of better physical health. Also, some physical ills have their origins, at least partially, in emotional disorders; the healing of emotional problems can sometimes radically improve or even completely heal biological illness.

This section describes inner healing.[2] By the term 'inner healing' I mean both spiritual and psychological healing; my approach here will be along the lines of the psychological, but without neglecting the spiritual.

Ordinarily, prayer for inner healing does not take place in a large group, although it can, but rather on a one-to-one basis, or with perhaps two people praying for the inner healing of a third. A confessor can pray for inner healing for a penitent during or immediately after the sacrament of penance. One can simply pray oneself for one's own inner healing – and this is the most common.

What is prayer for inner healing? All of us, at least sometimes, have experienced inner suffering, or conflicts, or strong and unreasonable anger or fear or sadness. We know from the gospels that Jesus can heal us, not only physically, but also interiorly, psychologically, emotionally, spiritually. We know, too, that prayers are answered.

Often the Lord will work through some people to heal others, for example, through psychological counselling. However, Jesus also heals simply in answer to prayer for inner healing. This means that we can pray for and with others that they be healed in their emotions, and it means that we ourselves can pray to be healed interiorly.

We know from psychology and psychiatry that much of what needs to be healed in us is buried beneath the level of consciousness. Interior suffering or stress or sadness frequently results from root problems or hurts or wounds or conflicts that are not conscious, that we are not aware of. We see only the tips of the icebergs that need to be melted. It is not necessary to know with precision what needs healing, although it helps. We can pray to be healed, interiorly, in our emotions, insofar as we are aware that we need healing, and then we can let the Lord take it from there and guide us to what we should do or pray for next.

Where do these – mostly unconscious – hurts come from? They come from the very beginning of our existence, from our earliest years, from our childhood and growing up, from the whole process of living. Some of them are so early and so deeply repressed that we can never get at them; but Our Lord sees them all and can heal them all. Many interior wounds, both conscious and buried, result from poor or inadequate home life in childhood, from negative aspects of school life, from setbacks in childhood or in later life. In many cases, things have been done to people which ought never to have been done, a lot of suffering was caused, and healing is needed.

In general, and without making rigid classifications, we can distinguish three kinds of prayer for inner healing. We can pray for healing of the heart, of the affective drives; often the reasons for a negative state are unknown, or vague, or dispersed, but the affectivity seems disturbed in such a way that the resulting emotions tend to block progress in union with God. Examples are a relative incapacity to love or to receive the love of others, a timidity that severely limits communication with others, general depression. Such problems no doubt have their roots, at least partly, in buried memories, but often these memories are inaccessible. Sometimes, especially in the case of depressive personalities, looking for root memories can bring to the surface psychological conflicts that might better remain unconscious or that require the attention of a psychologist or psychiatrist.

Secondly, we can pray for liberation from a habit or a tendency that goes against progress in union with God. For example, we can pray that the Lord free us from excessive suspiciousness, or from selfishness, or from fear, or from patterns of undesirable behaviour, or from depression.

Another way to pray for inner healing is to pray for healing of memories. We can simply ask the Lord to bring to mind any past memory or memories that he wants to heal. And then we can ask him to heal that memory. Memories to be healed might be childhood memories of an over-strict father or a possessive mother, or of an alcoholic or otherwise ill parent, or of poverty, or loneliness, or fear of a certain teacher, or shame at being too fat, or of an accident or physical abuse or a thousand other things. These trouble-causing memories will be found to contain one or more of the four typical reactions to stress: anger (or bitterness or resentment), fear (or withdrawal), anxiety, or guilt feelings.

In prayer, I can take the Lord's hand and let him walk back in time, in my own personal history, to the time and place where I was hurt. I can ask him to be present in that hurtful situation – in the home, or in the classroom, or on the playground – filling it with his healing love. And I can

9

ask him to take the pain out of the memory, to remove all fear and anxiety and guilt and anger associated with that memory, and to fill the places where they were with his love, healing the memory. I pray not that the memory disappear, but that its meaning be changed so that I can praise God and even thank him for what happened, knowing that he writes straight with crooked lines and that the healed memory will mean the conversion of past hurts into greater understanding of the hurts of others, into a broader and deeper compassion, or into some other positive force.

## The conditions of inner healing

What do we need to do to dispose ourselves prayerfully to let the Lord heal us interiorly? What are the conditions of inner healing? There are three: faith – that we believe in Jesus' power to heal us personally; repentance; and forgiveness of others.

God acts in and through Jesus. And he asks us to believe not only in his love but also in his power, for his love is powerful and it heals. Believing in Jesus' love for me is one thing; more is needed – to believe in the force of his love, in the healing power of his compassion for me personally. The healing power of the humanity of Jesus is surely not less than it was when he helped people during his public ministry; if anything, it is greater after his resurrection. And he has promised us that he hears and answers our prayers.

The second condition of inner healing is repentance. This includes the renunciation of sin and a conversion, a turning towards God in humility to accept his mercy and forgiving love. It helps to remember that the Lord came to save not the just but sinners, and that my very sinfulness attracts his loving compassion, that the dark side of myself, that I find hard to accept, he accepts totally and lovingly, and that my

10

very weakness is the opening in me to him and to his saving strength which is made perfect in my weakness.

I want to accept the Lord's forgiveness and to let him heal me. This means encountering him in prayer in terms of the disorder in my life; it means coming before the merciful Lord as the sinful, hurt, disordered person that I am. I want to be aware, in the light of the Lord's love, of my sinfulness, of the dark side of myself, aware that I am held captive in a sinful frame of reference so that he can minister to the effects of sin in me – original sin, my personal sins, and the sins and imperfections of others. To do this, I want to be centred not on myself and my sins, nor on some experience that I want to have of the Lord, but on the forgiving Lord himself, going to him, small, lowly, and simply, like a child, knowing that the initiative is his, not mine, knowing that he called me to be forgiven and healed before I ever thought of it myself.

The third condition of inner healing is that we forgive others. Failure to forgive other persons the pain and the hurt that they have caused me can block me, can close me to the healing power of Jesus. The resentment or the anger that I feel towards a person who has hurt me can act as a hard shell around the inner wound that that person caused. That hard casing of resentment or bitterness can screen the hurt from Jesus' healing power.

Inner healing of the emotions depends to a great extent on reconciliation with God. It depends on repentance for sins and God's consequent forgiveness of those sins. Repentance and acceptance of God's mercy in reconciliation with him is a kind of inner healing, a spiritual healing. And it is closely connected with emotional healing and can often lead to it. On the other hand, little healing of the emotions by the power of the Holy Spirit is possible unless repentance and reconciliation with God are present.

11

However, the grace of repentance frequently depends on my forgiving others. God can forgive us only insofar as we forgive others; and so we pray 'forgive us our trespasses as we forgive those who trespass against us'; 'forgive us our sins as we forgive those who sin against us'. If I do not forgive others, the hurt or bitterness, or resentment, or anger inside me keeps me from that repentance and openness to God that are necessary for my acceptance of God's forgiveness and so for the healing of my emotions and feelings.

Sometimes our failure to forgive is buried, lies below the level of awareness. We think, or we take for granted, that we have forgiven others; but our resentment and unforgiveness remain inside us, not conscious. This is why it is often important to forgive those who have hurt us, whether they intended to or not, even when we are not aware of any bitterness or lack of forgiveness on our part.

And many of us need to forgive ourselves for our sins, our mistakes and our failures. I need to accept Jesus' and the Father's total and unconditional acceptance of me; accepting God's acceptance of me, I can accept myself. Our Lord loves me not in spite of the dark side of myself but partly because of it; he came to save not the just but sinners, and my sinfulness attracts his loving compassion. Accepting his compassionate and loving forgiveness and acceptance of me, I can forgive myself.

Sometimes we need to forgive God. Obviously, there is no fault at all in God. Nevertheless, I might feel, in a vague way, some resentment against God for my own limitations or failures, for illness or an accident, for the death of someone I love, or for circumstances of my life. God wants me to forgive him, so that I can get over my resentment, accept his love better, and be healed.

## Praying for inner healing

Perhaps now, reading this chapter, or later in a moment of tranquillity, you can pray for inner healing.

1. The first step is to ask, with as much faith as you have, that the Lord heal you interiorly:

> Lord, you have told us to ask and we will receive, to seek and we will find, to knock and you will open the door to us. I ask you now for inner healing. Heal me, make me whole. I trust in your personal love for me and in the healing power of your compassion.

2. The second step is repentance, a turning to the Lord for forgiveness. Coming into the light of his love and understanding, I am free to see myself as I really am and to become more aware of the sin, the disorder, and the hurts and the wounds inside me. I am free, in the Lord's love, to see better my need for forgiveness and for inner healing.

> Lord, I am sorry for all my sins, and I trust in your mercy. With your help, I renounce my sins and any sinful patterns in my life; I renounce everything that in any way opposes you. I accept with all my heart your forgiving love. And I ask you for the grace to be aware of the disorder in my inner self, to experience my own interior disorder with my wounds and hurts and sinfulness.
>
> Guide me in this prayer; show me what to pray for and how to pray. Bring to my mind whatever pain or hurts you want me to ask you to heal.

3. Now, see what problem or painful experience comes to mind, and pray for healing regarding that problem or that memory. (If more than one thing comes to mind, take them one at a time.) It might be a failure or a broken friendship

or the loss of a person you love. It could be something in childhood, such as a less than perfect relationship with your father or your mother. It could be present anger or depression or some undesirable behaviour pattern.

Pray in your own words, lifting up the hurt or the painful memory or the problem to the Lord for healing. Pray simply like a child.

4. Forgive everyone involved, praying for them by name and telling the Lord that, with his help, you forgive each one. Imagine the person to be forgiven and, in your imagination, put your arms around that person and say, 'I forgive you'. Then see the Lord in your imagination, his arms outstretched to embrace you both, and – with one arm around the person you have forgiven – walk with that person into the Lord's arms and let him forgive you both and reconcile you to each other and to himself.

5. Picture in your imagination the situation the problem goes back to, or the place of the hurtful memory. Picture the Lord in that place and situation, filling it with his healing love, being with you there. And ask him to heal you, again praying simply and in your own words.

### *Inner healing in context*

Inner healing can take place in personal prayer when a person prays alone; it can take place while praying for inner healing with one or two other persons; and it can take place in a group where inner healing is prayed for. Privileged situations for healing to take place are the sacraments, especially confession of sins, the anointing of the sick, and the eucharist, celebration of the Lord's supper. When I confess my sins, I can express sorrow for them, receive God's pardon and his peace, and also pray for and receive healing of the wounds and hurts that might be connected with the sins

14

I confessed or that might be at the root of the sinful tendencies that resulted in those sins. The sacrament of the anointing of the sick is not only in preparation for the life to come, but for forgiveness of sins and for both bodily and inner healing. The eucharist, especially, is the sacrament of the healing of personal relationships, of being made more one in Jesus through sharing the same bread. And, in general, the prayer '. . . but only say the word and I shall be healed' is meant to be said in faith, with a faith that is hopeful, that *expects* (for hope is expectation in faith) healing to take place.

So far I have considered inner healing somewhat as an isolated action, a result of an explicit prayer for healing. Inner healing can also be situated within the total process of encountering the Lord; seen in this way, inner healing can be understood more realistically. Furthermore, it can be understood better as an integral part of growth in union with the Lord, as a condition of deep conversion, and as leading to service.

The story of the meeting between Jesus and the Samaritan woman (John 4.7-42) casts light on the place of inner healing as part of the process of prayer. The process begins with a journey, a movement towards the Lord, ending with a stopping short in his presence. There takes place a bringing into awareness of the disorder in the woman's life and the beginning of a re-ordering. This incipient re-ordering itself initiates a conversion process that clarifies the woman's understanding of herself – as a sinner and as called. In turn, conversion brings her closer to the Lord and gives her a new freedom which takes shape in mission; she goes out to the other Samaritans with the good news, having accepted a call that names her personally and that goes beyond that to become a call to go to others, a sending to bring the good news of the Lord. The Samaritan woman understands better who she is ('He told me all I ever did') in

15

her acceptance of Jesus ('Could he be the Christ?'), and goes out to spread the good news ('Come, see . . .').

The healing of Peter's mother-in-law (Mark 1.29-31) shows the same connection between healing and service. 'The fever left her; and she served them.' The received healing becomes a new freedom to serve. It occurs commonly, when a person receives a healing from the Lord, that that person looks for some form of service to give shape to his gratitude and to his freedom.

# 2

## *Crying out to the Lord*

From the cross, Jesus cries out to the Father, 'Eloi, Eloi, lama sabachthani?' ('My God, my God, why have you forsaken me?' – Mark 15.34; Matthew 27.46): he prays from the heart, expressing how he feels. Completely broken down, dying, incapable of putting words together to form a prayer, he falls back on a prayer he knows by heart and speaks the first verse of Psalm 22. Psalm 22 well expresses Jesus' situation on the cross. It is a prayer that fits so well as to be prophetic of the passion:

> But I am a worm, and no man; scorned by men
> and despised by all the people.
> All who see me mock at me, they make mouths
> at me, they wag their heads;
> 'He committed his cause to the Lord; let him
> deliver him, let him rescue him, for he
> delights in him!'(vv. 6-8)
> They have pierced my hands and feet (v. 16).
> They divide my garments among them, and for
> my raiment they cast lots (v. 18).

The gospel-writers, well aware of Jesus' suffering and death as fulfilling the scriptures, consciously point out the fulfilment of Psalm 22. But this hardly accounts for the prayer on Jesus' lips; he prays somehow not to prove that he fulfils prophecies, but to cry out to God. He laments, complains, cries out to his Father for deliverance – not with despair, but in extreme distress. The answer to Jesus' cry, his deliverance, comes in the resurrection.

Psalm 22 is a prayer of lament, a kind of prayer that, sadly, we have neglected in Christianity in recent times. Contemporary scholarship, in its rediscovery of the importance of the prayer of lament in the Bible and in theology,[1] points up the need to revalidate lamentation as a Christian form of prayer.

### Psalms of lament

Several psalms are lamentations, prayers of lament, and they have a common prayer structure.[2] The pattern usually begins with a calling to God or a preliminary prayer of petition: Psalm 22, 'My God, my God'; Psalm 69, 'Save me, O God'; Psalm 42, 'As a hart longs for flowing streams, so longs my soul for you, O God.' Psalm 102 has a longer introduction:

> Hear my prayer, O Lord, let my cry come to you!
> Do not hide your face from me in the day of my
>     distress!
> Incline your ear to me; answer me speedily in
>     the day when I call (vv. 1-2).

There follows a description of the situation characterized by a complaint against God – a lament directed to God. For example, Psalm 22 continues, 'Why have you forsaken me? O my God, I cry by day, but you do not answer; and by night, but find no rest,' and goes on to detail the plight of the author, 'I am poured out like water . . . my strength is dried up like a potsherd . . . you lay me down in a deathly dust' (vv. 14-15). And Psalm 69 begins:

> Save me, O God!
> For the waters have come up to my neck.

18

I sink in deep mire, where there is no foothold;
I have come into deep waters, and the flood
   sweeps over me.
I am weary with my crying; my throat is parched.
My eyes grow dim with waiting for my God (vv. 1-3).

Psalm 44, after describing in some detail the trouble the psalmist finds himself in, and after complaining strongly to God, finally shouts, 'Wake up! Why, O Lord, are you asleep? Wake up!' (v. 23).

The complaining is typically followed by a turning to God in confidence, a statement of trust in God's goodness, justice and power. Almost always, this trust appears as an act of the will, unfelt in the emotions, a hanging on to God against all feelings and in all circumstances. Psalm 22:

Yet you are holy, enthroned on the praises of
   Israel.
In you our fathers trusted; they trusted and
   you delivered them.
To you they cried, and were saved; in you they
   trusted and were not disappointed (vv. 3-5).

Psalm 130 makes its hope explicit:

If you, O Lord, should mark iniquities, Lord,
   who could stand? . . .
I wait for the Lord, my soul waits, and in his
   word I hope;
My soul waits for the Lord more than watchmen for
   the morning, more than watchmen for the morning.
O Israel, hope in the Lord (vv. 3-7).

Psalm 39 is the lament of one who sees this life as a pilgrimage towards the promised future; life is fleeting, and we are sojourners on earth. Therefore: 'And now, Lord, what am I waiting for? I put my hope in you' (v. 8). This hopeful turning to God leads naturally into a prayer of petition, a cry for help. Psalm 22 prays, 'Hasten to my aid! Deliver my soul from the sword . . .' (vv. 19-20). Psalm 69 continues its metaphor of mire and waters:

> . . . Rescue me from sinking in the mire;
> Let me be delivered from my enemies and from
>     the deep waters.
> My eyes grow dim with waiting for my God (vv. 1-3).
> Let not the flood sweep over me, or the deep
>     swallow me up, or the pit close its mouth
>     over me (v. 15).

Psalm 102 uses strong poetic images:

> My days pass away like smoke, and my bones burn
>     like a furnace.
> My heart is smitten like grass, and withered;
>     I forget to eat my bread.
> Because of my loud groaning, my bones cleave to
>     my flesh.
> I am like a vulture of the wilderness, like an
>     owl of the waste places;
> I lie awake, I am like a lonely bird on a
>     housetop (vv. 3-7).

Psalm 142 prays to be brought out of prison and to be delivered from persecutors (vv. 6-7); Psalm 88 appeals to God's goodness and prays, 'I spread out my hands to you. . . . In the morning my prayer comes before you' (vv. 9,13).

Often, psalms of lament conclude with a promise of praise or thanksgiving: 'Surely the righteous shall give praise to your name' (Psalm 140); 'Hope in God, for I shall again praise him, my help and my God' (Psalm 42).

The psalm of lament, then, does not stop at lamentation. It complains to God, but then transcends any tendency to self-pity by appealing to him who can remove the suffering. Complaint, turning to God in trust, crying out to him for help – these are the basic and inseparable elements of the psalms of lament; the complaint moves easily and naturally into a trustful turning to the Lord and so into asking to be saved. The psalm of lament is a prayer for healing that ends in thanking and praising God for his healing power. This final praise and thanksgiving indicate that an interior change takes place in the course of the prayer, that the beginning of healing takes place or is at least implied right in the prayer itself.

### Lament in the Old Testament

The psalms of lament form the heart of the Old Testament tradition of lament, and contain most of its highly developed expressions. However, the prayer of lament is an integral part of the prayer tradition of the whole Old Testament. The two basic categories of Old Testament piety, covenant and exodus, give the people of Israel the right to lament – because God is their God and they are his people – and establish the lament to God as the beginning of salvation. The exodus begins with the Lord's response to the crying out of his people.

Perhaps the oldest text in the Bible, the certainly ancient cultic formula of Deuteronomy 26.5-10, contains a summary of the exodus experience in the form of a prayer of gratitude:

A wandering Aramean was my father; and he went down into Egypt and sojourned there, few in number; and he became a nation, great, mighty, and populous. And the Egyptians treated us harshly, and afflicted us,

21

and laid upon us hard bondage. Then we cried to the Lord the God of our fathers, and the Lord heard our voice, and saw our affliction, our toil, and our oppression; and the Lord brought us out of Egypt with a mighty hand and an outstretched arm, with great terror, with signs and wonders; and he brought us into this place and gave us this land, a land flowing with milk and honey. And behold, now I bring the first of the fruit of the ground, which you, O Lord, have given me.

This summary of the first fifteen chapters of the Book of Exodus situates the place of the prayer of lament in the spirituality of the Old Testament and underlines its significance. 'Then we cried to the Lord' – this phrase establishes the exodus itself as a response to prayer, to the cry of the people to God for help. The anguished cry for help, more than an historical event, constitutes a dimension of Israel's relationship with God; lament is an important part of what happens between God and his people in the history of the covenant relationship. Over and over in Israel's history, the people cry out to the Lord, and he hears their voice and sees their affliction and 'is moved to compassion by their groaning' (Judg. 2.18).

The pattern is always the same: people, in suffering and anguish, cry out to the Lord for help; the Lord hears their cry and brings them out of their suffering and into a new and blessed situation; the people rejoice in the Lord, praising and thanking him. Cain laments, 'My punishment is greater than I can bear,' and the Lord answers, 'Not so,' and puts a saving mark on him (Gen. 4.13). Hagar and her son lament; the Lord hears the boy's weeping and reassures Hagar; 'and God was with the lad, and he grew up' (Gen. 21.16-20). Samson, ready to die of thirst, calls on the Lord; water gushes forth out of a hollow place, 'and when he drank, his spirit returned, and he revived' (Judg. 15.18-19). When the tribe of Benjamin seems lost to Israel, the people lift up their voices to God and weep bitterly before him (Judg. 21.2), and he answers their prayer. Hannah cries out to God, weeping bitterly, complaining of her inability to have a child; 'and the Lord remembered her; and in due time Hannah conceived and bore a son, and she called his name Samuel' (I Sam. 1.10-20). Samuel, explaining to the people that the Lord has given them Saul as king, recounts the times Israel cried out and was delivered by the Lord: '. . . your fathers cried to the Lord, and the Lord sent Moses and Aaron, who brought forth your fathers out of Egypt. . . . And they cried to the Lord, and the Lord sent Jerubbaal and Barak, and Jephthah, and Samuel, and delivered you . . .' (I Sam. 12.6-17). Solomon, praying at the dedication of the temple, asks the Lord to hear any laments of the people offered in the temple, and to forgive them their sins, save them from their afflictions, and restore them to well-being (II Chron. 6.24-31).

The outstanding example of individual lamentation is the Book of Job. Job's lament consists of bitter complaining to God against God. He refuses his friends' ideas that his suffering is punishment for sin or that it has any rational explanation. He has no way to understand his situation; it is absurd, and the philosophical arguments of Job's friends only highlight the absurdity. Finally, the Lord responds to Job, and Job declares humbly to God that he has spoken about matters too deep for him, and that he repents 'in dust and ashes' (Job 42.1-6). 'And the Lord restored the fortunes of Job' (Job 42.10).

The lament for the people, for the nation, is a common form of prayer of lament. Psalms 79 and 80 are psalms of lament for Israel, begging the Lord for his own name's sake for forgiveness and liberation (79.9), not to be angry for ever

(79.5; 80.4), but to let his face shine that his people may be saved (80.3, 7 and 19). The exodus begins with a lament of the people that the Lord listens to: 'Then the Lord said, "I have seen the affliction of my people who are in Egypt, and have heard their cry because of their taskmasters . . ." ' (Exod. 3.7). And lament continues during the exodus in the form of the murmuring of the people. National prayers of lament are frequent throughout Israel's history; they ask for deliverance from enemy forces, from natural disasters, and for the restoration of Israel. For example, the people of Judah lament to the Lord:

> Look down from heaven and see . . .
> Where are your zeal and your power?
> The yearning of your heart and your compassion
>     are held from me (Isa. 63.15; the whole prayer
>     is Isa. 63.15–64.12).

A special type of national lament is the prayer of lament for the people by a mediator. The mediator cries out to God for his or her people, and becomes instrumental in God's saving response to that prayer of lament. Moses laments, complains to God, prays for God's people in Exodus: 'O Lord, why does your wrath burn hot against your people . . . ? Why should the Egyptians say, "With evil intent did he bring them forth, to slay them in the mountains" . . . ?' The text continues: 'And the Lord repented of the evil which he thought to do to his people' (Exod. 32.11-14; see also Deut. 9.25-29; Exod. 32.30-32; Exod. 33.12-19; Num. 11.1-23; 12.13; 14.11-19; Josh. 7.6-9). Gideon complains to the angel of the Lord, who has told him that the Lord is with him:

'Pray, sir, if the Lord is with us, why then has all this befallen us? And where are all his wonderful deeds

24

which our fathers recounted to us?' . . . And the Lord turned to him and said, 'Go in this might of yours and deliver Israel from the hand of Midian; do I not send you?' And he said to him, 'Pray, Lord, how can I deliver Israel? Behold my clan is the weakest in Manasseh, and I am the least in my family.' And the Lord said to him, 'But I will be with you . . .' (Judg. 6.13-16).

David, conscious that his people are suffering the plague because of David's own sin, speaks to the Lord: 'Lo, I have sinned, and I have done wickedly; but these sheep, what have they done?' (II Sam. 24.17). He offers 'burnt offerings and peace offerings', and the plague is averted (II Sam. 24.25). At the moment of the evening incense offering in the Jerusalem temple, Judith, prostrate, cries out in a loud voice to the Lord in a beautiful prayer of lament for her people (Judith, ch. 9), and the Lord uses her to deliver Israel in a victory that she celebrates in a joyful canticle of praise and thanksgiving (Judith 15.14–16.17). Daniel seeks the Lord 'by prayer and supplications with fasting and sackcloth and ashes, praying for forgiveness and salvation for the people' (Dan. 9.3-19). Ezra pleads for the people, newly re-established in Israel after their exile (Ezra 9; Neh. 9.6-38). One of the most beautiful prayers of lament on behalf of the community is the last chapter of Jeremiah's Lamentations; it ends in a prayer for reconciliation and inner healing:

> Alas that we ever sinned!
> At this our heart has become sick;
>> These things have darkened our sight.
> On Mount Zion, lying desolate, foxes prowl.
> Yet you, Lord, rule for ever;
>> Your throne is eternal.
> Why do you never think of us?
>> Why abandon us so long?

> Bring us back to you, Lord, and we will return.
>
> Make our days as they were before.
>
> But instead you have completely rejected us;
>
> You have been very angry with us (Lam. 5.16-22).[3]

The mediator prays, cries out, that the people be saved, and then, somehow, becomes part of the process of salvation. This is clearest in the case of the Suffering Servant of Second Isaiah, who answers Israel's complaint that 'The Lord has forsaken me, my Lord has forgotten me' (Isa. 49.14) with a message of consoling hope and with a suffering intercession that bears 'the sin of many', and makes 'intercession for the transgressors' (Isa. 53.12).

The passion and death of Jesus follow in detail the songs of the Suffering Servant, with whom Jesus explicitly identifies himself, particularly in his predictions of his suffering and death. The long Old Testament tradition of the mediator's prayer of lament for the people, a tradition culminating in the laments of Jeremiah and in the mediation of the Suffering Servant of Second Isaiah, is gathered up in the intercessory act of Jesus in laying down his life.

## The nature of the prayer of lament

Three things need to be observed about the tradition of lament in the Old Testament. The first is that the lament is hopeful; it looks to the future, to liberation, to healing. It is not a lament of mourning or regret that looks backwards to past loss or failure, but a lament of affliction that cries out to God for freedom from the affliction.

Secondly, the prayer of lament knows no reasons. No attempt is made to argue for deliverance on the basis of the merits of the afflicted. The appeal is directly to the Lord's compassion. The need is shown to him; he is simply asked to look at the wounds, at the suffering, and to act in his loving mercy and faithful compassion. The Lord acts because of his own goodness, his own holiness:

> Thus says the Lord God: It is not for your sake, O house of Israel, that I am about to act, but for the sake of my holy name . . . I will vindicate the holiness of my great name . . . I will sprinkle clean water upon you, and you shall be clean from all your uncleannesses, and from all your idols I will cleanse you. A new heart I will give you, and a new spirit I will put within you; and I will take out of your flesh the heart of stone and give you a heart of flesh. And I will put my spirit within you . . . (Ezek. 36.22-27).

And his action in response to cries for help is to save and to heal – both physically and interiorly – not only to forgive sins.

Finally, something must be said about the place of sin in the prayer of lament. The salvation asked for is rarely salvation from sin. Sometimes, however, it is, as in Psalm 51, the great prayer for forgiveness and spiritual healing, and in David's prayer for forgiveness of his sin (II Sam. 24.10-14). The prayer of lament asks for salvation *now*, for help in this life, for freedom from enemies, for the healing of sickness, for deliverance from hunger and thirst. This fact has important implications for our understanding of prayer for healing and for our understanding of the meaning of the salvation that Jesus Christ won for us through his suffering and death.

### Prayer of lament in the New Testament

The most common prayer of lament in the gospels is the request, made to Jesus, for healing.

> And a leper came to him, and kneeling said to him, 'If you will, you can make me clean.' Moved with compassion,

he stretched out his hand and touched him, and said to him, 'I will; be clean.' And immediately the leprosy left him, and he was made clean (Mark 1.40-42).

The Canaanite woman begs Jesus for the healing of her daughter (Mark 7.25-30). Bartimaeus, the blind beggar, cries out, 'Jesus, Son of David, have mercy on me' over and over (Mark 10.46-52), just as the ten lepers call out, 'Jesus, Master, have mercy on us' (Luke 17.12-19). After Lazarus' death, Martha tells Jesus, 'Lord, if you had been here, my brother would not have died. And even now I know that whatever you ask from God, God will give you' (John 11.21-22).

Often, the 'prayer of lament' is simply the silent presence of suffering, either physical, as in the cure of Peter's mother-in-law's fever (Mark 1.30-31), or spiritual as well as physical, as in the forgiveness and healing of the paralytic lowered by his friends through a hole in the roof (Mark 2.3-12). Jesus sees the widow of Nain, has compassion on her, tells her not to weep, and raises up her dead son (Luke 7.12-15).

Jesus, in his teaching on prayer, encourages asking with faith and expecting to receive a positive answer to prayer of petition (e.g. Matt. 6.7-12; John 16.23-24). The parable of the unrighteous judge has as its point the efficacy of crying out to God; Jesus makes it explicit: 'And will not God vindicate his elect, who cry to him day and night? Will he delay long over them? I tell you, he will vindicate them speedily' (Luke 18.1-8).

Jesus himself cries out in lament to the Father in his agony in the garden and in praying the first verse of Psalm 22 on the cross. His other laments, however, seem to be in line with the Old Testament tradition of the lament of God. God laments for his people especially in the prophecies of

Jeremiah (see 8.5-7; 12.7-13; 15.5-9; 18.13-17). At the beginning of the book of Isaiah, God complains: 'Sons I have reared and brought up, but they have rebelled against me' (1.2). The whole book of Hosea is based on God's lament over his people: 'The Lord said to Hosea, "Go, take a prostitute for a wife, because the country is committing fornication by forsaking the Lord" ' (Hos. 1.2). This tradition of God's lamenting over his people, his disappointment and anger expressed to Moses during the exodus (e.g. Num. 14.11), down through the prophetic books, seems to find its final expression in the laments of God become man. Jesus weeps over Jerusalem, 'How often would I have gathered your children together as a hen gathers her brood under her wings, and you would not! Behold, your house is forsaken' (Luke 13.34-35); and he laments its future destruction (Luke 21.23). He complains about the lack of faith of his disciples (e.g. Matt. 17.17), and he upbraids cities that will not repent (Matt. 11.20-24).

## Crying out to the Lord

When we need help, we can, and should, cry out to the Lord, not afraid to express how we feel, openly speaking to him our pain or resentment or fear or sadness. One way to come to the Lord lamenting is to choose a prayer of lament from the Psalms, or from some other book in the Old Testament, and say it slowly with the present situation in mind. Another way is to pray in your own words, following the structure of the psalms of lament:

1. Calling out to the Lord; for example, 'Jesus, Son of David, have mercy on me', or 'Out of the depths I cry to you, O Lord'.
2. Lamenting, complaining, expressing just how you feel to the Lord.

29

3. An act of trust, of confidence in the Lord's personal love, and in the saving power of his love.

4. Asking to be saved or to be healed, or that another person for whom you are praying be helped by the Lord; it is a good idea to ask explicitly, to describe in a prayer of petition the kind of help you are praying for.

5. Thanking and praising the Lord for his compassion, for the saving power of his love. This can take the form of a promise of praise and thanksgiving, or of praise and thanksgiving right away, in anticipation, as a form of trust in the Lord's response.

The psalms, including those of lament, have always been an important part of the church's worship,[4] as they still are today. The psalms of lament make up part of the divine office, the official prayer of the church; and the Lamentations of Jeremiah are part of the Good Friday Liturgy. The church herself laments, and teaches us to cry out to the Lord. We can call out to God in trust, because the risen Jesus stands 'in the presence of God on our behalf' (Heb. 9.24), interceding for us, praying the lament of the mediator. We can cry out to the Father in his name, and to Jesus himself, who is our Saviour.

Lord, have mercy on us.

# 3

# *By his Wounds we are Healed*

The Christian tradition has always held that Jesus died not just for all people, but for each person as though that person were the only other person on earth. The mystery of the fact that God present in Jesus Christ loves each one of us personally, by name, without illusions and with total and unconditional acceptance, finds its centre in the cross: that Jesus loves me so much as to have died to save me. No one can love more than to lay down his life for his friend; the cross weighs Jesus' love for me, tells me its measure.

This is one side of the equation, the cross as the measure of love; the other side is the power of that love to heal and to save, the power of Jesus' suffering and death, the healing power of his cross. Prayerfully entering into the healing structure of the cross of Jesus, we can enter more deeply into his love, and live better his wisdom – which is the foolishness of the cross.

### *The cross as Jesus' experience of sin*

We can better understand the love of Jesus for each of us through trying to understand better his experience, what he underwent out of love for the Father and for his friends – that is, for each of us.[1] To see the suffering of Jesus as substitutionary, as vicarious suffering for our sins, does not fully explain the mystery of the cross.[2] But it is a truthful insight: that Jesus died for our sins, that he gave his life as a ransom for many, that one man died for the sake of the people. Jesus died for our sins, that is, he suffered the consequences of sin, and so experienced God's anger against him, the divine wrath against all sinfulness.

But is God really a God of anger? Does not Christianity overcome the 'just God' conception of the Old Testament in Jesus' teaching about the loving mercy of our Father? Marcion, the great second-century gnostic heretic, thought so, and rejected the Old Testament's just God of wrath for the New Testament's loving Father. The heresy lay in thinking the two contradictory. They are not: 'In God there are mercy and wrath, support and pardon, but against the impious he unleashes his anger' (Ecclus 16.12). The Lord strikes out against sinfulness, and – at the same time – purifies and saves those who trust in him:

> 'Behold, the eyes of the Lord God are upon the sinful kingdom, and I will destroy it from the surface of the ground; except that I will not uttery destroy the house of Jacob,' says the Lord . . .

> 'I will restore the fortunes of my people Israel, and they shall rebuild the ruined cities . . .' (Amos 9.9,14).

> 'I will fulfil my words against this city for evil and not for good; . . . but I will deliver you on that day,' says the Lord (Jer. 39.16-17).

The first chapter of Paul's Letter to the Romans teaches that God's anger is revealed through God's leaving those who persist in sin to the consequences of those same sins (vv. 18-31). Sin contains the seed of its own punishment, and that punishment reveals the wrath of God against sin. The revelation of God's justice, the justice by which God makes us just, justifies us, is revealed in the death of Jesus Christ,

> . . . whom God put forward as an expiation by his blood, to be received by faith. This was to show God's righteousness, because in his divine forbearance he had passed over former sins; it was to prove at the present time that he himself is righteous and that he justifies whoever has faith in Jesus (Rom. 3.25-26).

Through faith in Jesus Christ who died for us, we receive, in God's justice, forgiveness, justification. We have, then, nothing to fear from God's anger nor from his justice. In his anger against sin, he saves us from it, and in his justice, out of love for us, he saves us to himself; all this because Jesus Christ suffered and died for our sins.

Jesus' experience, then, was one of being 'made sin' for us, of carrying our sins and the 'sin of the world'. He was without sin (John 8.46), but he was tried and tempted as we are (Heb. 4.15). 'He had to be made like his brethren in every respect . . . to make expiation for the sins of the people' (Heb. 2.17-18). God, 'sending his own Son in the likeness of sinful flesh and for sin, condemned sin in the flesh' (Rom. 8.3). 'For our sake,' God 'made him to be sin who knew no sin, so that in him we might become the righteousness of God' (II Cor. 5.21).

Jesus' suffering and death expiate our sins. In the Bible, expiation is not the undergoing of punishment for sin, nor is it the mere appeasement of an angry God by an act of sacrifice. Primarily, expiation means the annihilation of sin, the destruction of sin, by a sacrificial act. 'Expiation does not act upon God himself, but upon the sinner inasmuch as it purifies him from sin.'[3] Dying, Jesus triumphs over death and so over sin and its consequences, for 'the sting of death is sin'; 'O death, where is your sting?' (I Cor. 15.56a,55b).

33

None of this means anything, of course, if we fail to understand the cross as an act of love, both on the part of the Father who sent his only Son to save us, and on Jesus' part, who lays down his life in love. Jesus' expiation is done for love and in love: 'In this is love, not that we loved God but that he loved us and sent his Son to be the expiation for our sins' (I John 4.10).

If God is for us, who is against us? He who did not spare his own Son but gave him up for us all, will he not also give us all things with him? . . . Who shall separate us from the love of Christ? . . . We are more than conquerors through him who loved us. For I am sure that neither death, nor life, nor angels, nor principalities, nor things present, nor things to come, nor powers, nor height, nor depth, nor anything else in all creation, will be able to separate us from the love of God in Christ Jesus our Lord (Rom. 8.31-39; see Rom. 5.6-8; John 3.16-17; II Cor. 5.15).

This said, let us examine the gospels to try to enter into the interior experience of Jesus, his psychological experience, what he felt.

### Jesus' psychological experience of the cross

Jesus foresaw and even predicted his own suffering and death. He accepted the brutal torture and ugly death without flinching and, above all, with his eyes open, not denying to himself nor to others what the future held.

And he began to teach them that the Son of man must suffer many things, and be rejected by the chief priests and the scribes, and be killed, and after three days rise again. And Peter took him, and began to rebuke him (Mark 8.31-33).

34

Jesus' rebuke of Peter, 'Get behind me, Satan; for you are not on the side of God, but of men' (Mark 8.33), expresses Jesus' resistance to the temptation to deny the reality of what is coming. He rejects, strongly, the temptation; and he encourages his followers to have that same clear-minded realism and to take up the cross and follow him (8.34-38). He predicts his passion again (9.30-32), and a third time, describing in more detail what will happen: his condemnation to death in Jerusalem, where they are headed; his consignment to the Roman forces of occupation; the mocking and the scourging (10.32-34). He foretells Judas' betrayal and Peter's denial, accepting both with resignation and a certain security (14.18,30).

In the context of his imminent torture and death, his anger against the kind of sinful blindness and crassness that is to crucify him appears as natural, healthy and certainly understandable. We recognize Jesus' unusual behaviour in violently driving the buyers and sellers out of the Temple as normal, not as deviant conduct; the Temple is being profaned just as the new temple, his own body, will very soon be profaned and hideously mistreated (Mark 11.15-18). Luke situates the cleaning out of the Temple just after Jesus' messianic entry into Jerusalem, as do Mark and Matthew, and immediately after his weeping over Jerusalem, so highlighting the pathos of his anger. In the light of the cross, Jesus' anger against the blind hypocrisy and resistance of the leaders of Israel can be seen as anger against that very sinfulness and darkness whose hour is coming shortly on Calvary.

Jesus knows what Israel's religious leaders are plotting against him, but he does not give in at all. He does not negotiate with the scribes and Pharisees or with the priests; he does not try to make a bargain. This uncompromising fidelity to the truth he proclaims and to the Father's loving will continues throughout the last supper and the passion. Before Annas and Caiaphas, Jesus does not defend himself, does not bargain. He stands silent in front of Herod, and does no miracle or feat that might help his cause. He refuses to negotiate with Pilate. What seems, in all this, to be stoicism is really the refusal of the temptation to bargain or to negotiate in the face of his suffering and death.

In the agony in the garden of Gethsemane, this same inner strength crumbles and dissolves, leaving only its source: adhesion to the Father's will. It reappears after Jesus' prayer in the garden as he rises from prayer and meets the armed men who have come to take him prisoner. What happened in the agony in the garden? What did Jesus experience there? He describes it himself: 'My soul is very anguished, even to death' (Mark 14.34); he is 'greatly distressed and troubled' (Mark 14.33). In other words, Jesus suffers not only fear, but severe depression. Luke's gospel describes Jesus' condition with the sentence: 'And being in an agony, he prayed more earnestly; and his sweat became like great drops of blood falling down upon the ground' (Luke 22.44). Sweating blood, perspiring mixed water and blood, is a symptom of a total physical and psychological breakdown, of an extremely grave depression which ordinarily ends in death.

And yet, Jesus somehow works through that severe depression in his prayer in Gethsemane. His interior resistance and revulsion to the passion lead him to cry out: 'Abba, Father, all things are possible to you; remove this cup from me' (Mark 14.36a). The prospect of drinking the cup of God's anger, of the divine wrath and judgment against sin, forces Jesus into a complete breakdown, into a killing depression. In agony, he continues to pray: 'Not my will, but yours be done' (Mark 14.36b). Centring himself and his prayer on this, that the Father's will be done, Jesus pulls himself together enough to be prepared to meet the men coming to arrest him.

The fruit of this suffering and of this acceptance of the Father's will is a compassion so great as to be nearly unbelievable. Jesus' first act after his agony is to heal the ear of the slave of the high priest (Luke 22.51). Nailed to the cross, he forgives the very people who are murdering him, praying that the Father forgive them, and even excusing them in his prayer (Luke 23.34). One of the thieves crucified with him asks to be remembered; Jesus forgives him and promises him Paradise that same day (Luke 23.42-43). He shows compassion for his mother, putting her in the care of John (John 19.26-27).

Shortly before Jesus dies, he cries out to the Father: 'My God, my God, why have you abandoned me?' (Mark 15.34). God feels abandoned by God; dying, practically incapable of prayer, he cries out in lament to his Father. God is dying, abandoned by God. That death is an act of love by Jesus for us and for the Father; and the Father gives Jesus up to death in an act of love for us and for Jesus. Their love for one another here becomes radical sacrifice. And that mutual love is the Holy Spirit, whose name is Love, and who is poured into our hearts by Jesus and his Father. Love gives meaning to the sacrifice.

Finally, Jesus gives a loud cry, 'Father, into your hands I commend my spirit,' and dies (Luke 23.46). Feeling completely abandoned, he abandons himself in death to his Father. The prayer, 'into your hands I commend my spirit,' is from a psalm of lament, Psalm 31.5. It probably formed a part of a common Jewish death-bed prayer.[4]

John's gospel reports two other exclamations of Jesus in his dying moments. Knowing that all is finished, Jesus says, 'I thirst'; as he dies, he says, 'It is finished' (19.28,30). Surely Jesus suffered from physical thirst. But John wants us to understand Jesus' thirst also in a spiritual sense; his thirst is his desire to give the living water of the Spirit.[5] The coming of the Spirit depends on Jesus' dying, and in giving up his spirit Jesus communicates to us, gives, his Spirit. This is the meaning of the blood and water that issue from the dead Jesus' side when it is pierced with the soldier's spear. The blood is the blood of Jesus' sacrifice, and the water symbolizes the Holy Spirit, the fountain of living water (see John 7.37-39; Zech. 12.10; 13.1); the water mixed with blood prefigures the permanent outpouring of the Spirit after Jesus' death.[6] And Jesus' Spirit is the Spirit of healing.

### The power of the cross to heal

It is easy to think of Jesus' suffering and death as punishment for sin, but this would be an error. God is not sadistic, and suffering is not a punishment he administers for sinning. Refusing God's love, separating from him, turning away from him – and these are what sin is – is its own punishment. Holding suffering to be punishment for sin sometimes masks an attitude of contempt toward the afflicted; they are viewed as suffering because they are sinners: 'They are too lazy to work, or too undisciplined to solve their problems, they get what is coming to them.' The attitude of the Father and of Jesus – they have the same attitude, for Jesus is the revelation of the Father – is just the opposite of contempt. It is compassion. Jesus, crucified outside the walls of the city, finds himself – rather chooses to be – identified with those outside the *cives*, outside civility and civilization, the outcasts, the forgotten, the despised, the hopelessly marginal and those beyond all margin. He suffers the treatment not of a common criminal but, worse, of an uncommon criminal, the charges trumped up, his trial a travesty, his torture brutally evil, and his execution a horror. And he takes upon himself the neediness of the abandoned, the poor, the oppressed, the suffering, and of all of us in whatever way we are consciously or unconsciously needy. He identifies with those who need to be saved so as to save them. He is 'made sin' for sinners. He becomes one with all of us who need healing so we may be healed.

He was crucified in weakness (II Cor. 13.4) so that we can glory in our own weakness and that the power of Christ may rest upon us; for when we are weak, we are strong (II Cor. 12.9). 'God chose what is weak in the world to shame the strong' (I Cor. 1.27), for 'the weakness of God is stronger than men' (I Cor. 1.25). God's power is made perfect in the weakness of Jesus crucified; it is through the power of the cross that the Father has chosen to reconcile all things to himself in Jesus Christ (Eph. 2.16; Col. 1.20), to knot things together making them whole, unifying and healing. Paul proclaims the power of the cross, and the cross as the power of God (I Cor. 1.17-18). This is not to take away from the power of the resurrection, but to say that for Paul 'the resurrection in fact begins at the moment of [Jesus'] death: . . . people are converted, the centurion confesses the faith, the Holy Spirit is poured out'.[7]

For John's gospel, too, Jesus' death rather than his resurrection is the completion of his work because by the cross the sources of eternal life are open to men; the cross has the power to save.

John's gospel proclaims the healing power of the cross by comparing it with the brazen serpent that Moses, following God's instructions, placed on a pole (Num. 21.4-9). Those who had been bitten by snakes looked at the serpent and were healed. 'Just as Moses lifted up the serpent in the wilderness, so must the Son of man be lifted up that whoever believes may have eternal life in him' (John 3.14-15).

39

And so John quotes Zechariah in reference to Jesus' side being opened by the spear: 'They shall look upon him whom they have pierced' (John 19.37; Zech. 12.10).

In the act of saving us, Jesus is mocked; the gospel writers do not want us to miss the irony of this mockery, unintentional irony for the mockers, but consciously included in the gospel.

> And those who passed by derided him, wagging their heads and saying, 'Aha! You who would destroy the temple and build it in three days, save yourself, and come down from the cross!' So also the chief priests mocked him to one another with the scribes, saying, 'He saved others; he cannot save himself . . .' (Mark 15.31).

There is a double irony. The religious leaders give testimony to Jesus' healings through their mocking words; 'he saved others' could have no other meaning than that Jesus healed sicknesses, cast out demons, raised the dead to life. Secondly, they make fun of Jesus for his weakness in the very hour that the power of God in Jesus saves the world. The saving and healing power of God cannot be dissociated from the cross of Jesus. Dennis Hamm has put the point concisely:

> The healing ministry of Jesus is fully understood only in the context of the saving death of Jesus. This is the clear message of the evangelists. Matthew, Mark, and Luke, in their descriptions of the crucifixion, present Jesus as the hanged healer. Jesus is taunted, 'He saved others; he cannot save himself'. The reference is, of course, to the healing ministry. And the evangelist includes the taunt, one suspects, because of the profound irony the words carry for the Christian reader: the hanged healer does indeed heal and save most deeply through his saving

death. Luke underscores this in his version of the second passion prediction (Luke 9.43b-44): 'But while they were all marvelling at everything he did (the healing of the demoniac has just been narrated), he said to his disciples, "Let these words sink into your ears, for the son of man is to be delivered into the hands of men." ' In other words, the appreciation of Jesus' healing ministry is not to be separated from the meaning of his passion and death.[8]

And this is the Christian tradition from the beginning, that by Jesus' wounds we are healed. The fourth song of Second Isaiah's Suffering Servant prophesies this:

> He was despised, the lowest of men: a man of
>     pains, familiar with disease,
> One from whom men avert their gaze –
>     despised, and we reckoned him as nothing.
> But it was our diseases that he bore,
>     our pains that he carried,
> While we counted him as one stricken,
>     touched by God with affliction.
> He was wounded for our rebellions, crushed
>     for our transgressions;
> The chastisement that reconciled us fell
>     upon him, and by his wounds we are
>     healed (Isa. 5.3-5).[9]

Matthew's gospel sees the healings of Jesus' public ministry as fulfilling the Suffering Servant prophecy: '. . . he cast out the spirits with a word, and healed all who were sick. This was to fulfil what was spoken by the prophet Isaiah, "He took our infirmities and bore our diseases" ' (Matt. 8.16b-17). Peter's first letter makes the application to the passion and death of Jesus: 'He himself bore our sins in his body on the tree, that we might die to sin and live to righteousness. By his wounds you have been healed' (2.24).

We can be healed by simply looking at Jesus, by looking upon 'him whom they have pierced', just as the Hebrews looked upon the raised up metal serpent and were healed. Also, we can pray for healing by prayerfully taking our own wounds into the structure of Jesus' passion and death. This is the purpose of the next chapter.

# 4

## *The Cross and Prayer for Inner Healing*

The cross is a statement to us, a 'word' about God and about ourselves; it reveals God, and in his light we too are revealed. The word of the cross reveals its power, the power made perfect in the weakness of the Crucified. Because the word of the cross speaks God's power in weakness, it is a word of wisdom that appears as foolishness (see I Cor. 1.18-25).

### *The foolishness of the cross*

To proclaim the cross appears foolish. Further, how could anyone be healed through the cross? To speak of the healing *power* of the cross seems a contradiction, for the cross at first glance means *weakness*. In the eyes of the world, the cross seems more than foolish, it appears as folly, as lunacy.

The Old Testament has a tradition of the wisdom of the wise seen by God as foolishness. The wisdom of Egypt appears at the exodus as stupidity: 'The princes of Zoan are utterly foolish; the wise counsellors of Pharaoh give stupid counsel' (Isa. 19.11a). Isaiah deplores those who think themselves wise, but who call good 'evil', and evil 'good' – 'Woe to those who are wise in their own eyes' (5.21) – as does Jeremiah – 'The wise men shall be put to shame, they shall be dismayed and taken; lo, they have rejected the

word of the Lord, and what wisdom is in them?' (8.9).
God's wisdom is infinitely above ours, beyond our logic:

> For my thoughts are not your thoughts,
> > neither are your ways my ways, says the Lord.
> For as the heavens are higher than the earth,
> > so are my ways higher than your ways and
> > my thoughts than your thoughts. (Isa. 55.8,9)

God's wisdom so far transcends ours that it can appear to us as foolishness. Job, unable to understand his miserable condition, complains loudly; the wisdom of his friends does not give him any answers. The Lord says, 'Shall a fault-finder contend with the Almighty', and Job puts his hand over his mouth and remains silent in face of what is so far above him that it seems completely unreasonable (Job 40.2-4). The human view is partial; it cannot know everything; 'even though a wise man claims to know, he cannot find it out' (Eccles. 8.17b).

> The kings of the earth set themselves, and the
> > rulers take counsel together, against the
> > Lord and his anointed . . .
> He who sits in the heavens laughs; the Lord
> > has them in derision . . .
> Now therefore, O kings, be wise . . .
> Serve the Lord with fear, with trembling (Psalm 2.2-11).

For Paul, the cross marks the definitive triumph of God's wisdom; the words of Isaiah, 'I will destroy the wisdom of the wise, and the cleverness of the clever I will thwart,' come true in a radical way in the suffering and death of Jesus, in the triumph of the cross (I Cor. 1.19; referring to Isa. 29.14). By the cross, God has made foolish the wisdom of the world (I Cor. 1.20b); and so the world's wisdom is foolishness to God (I Cor. 3.19a). Because of the foolishness of the cross, Paul becomes 'a fool for Christ's sake' (I Cor. 4.10).

So, too, in praying for inner healing, an attitude of 'being a fool for Christ' is a help. The qualities that go with being a fool – simplicity, openness, complete trust – make one more receptive to God's healing power. At the same time, inner healing is not a matter of scientific or psychological wisdom, nor of self-knowledge; it is a matter of grace, of the love of God poured into our hearts through the Holy Spirit, a love that heals us. The wisdom of God transcends human wisdom, goes so far beyond it as to look like lunacy, and so far that human wisdom itself is, by comparison, foolishness. The power of the inner healing that comes through prayer goes way beyond the power of psychology and of every merely human approach. It is a question of going to the Lord like a child, or like a fool, simply, and asking for healing. One way to do this is to put our own hurts into the context of the cross of Jesus so that they be healed. Saint Bonaventure has written:

The cross is our book, in which is written the whole wisdom of Christ . . . Only the cross can free you . . . The best thing is to meditate on the cross . . . So we should take up the cross of Christ as a book of wisdom, in which we see ourselves.[1]

Looking on 'him whom they have pierced' I can see his love for me, and – at the same time, in his light – see myself with my interior hurts, my weakness, my neediness. This 'looking' can free me, heal me, make me more whole.

*Praying about our hurts in the light of Jesus' passion*

The previous chapter described Jesus' psychological experience of his passion in eight steps:

45

1. Jesus foresaw his coming passion and death, and accepted it with open eyes.

2. Anger appears in his reaction, anger against the abuse of the Temple (a symbol of his body), and anger against the religious leaders who are plotting his murder.

3. He rejects the temptation to bargain with those who will kill him, just as later he refuses to negotiate with Annas, Caiaphas, Herod and Pilate.

4. He undergoes deathly depression in the garden of Gethsemane.

5. He embraces the Father's will, accepting his death, its form, its time, and the suffering leading up to it.

These five steps lead up to Jesus' death. The next three represent the psychological phases he passes through in his dying on the cross:

6. Compassion: he forgives his killers and the thief, and speaks compassionately to his mother and to John.

7. Feeling abandoned: 'My God, my God, why have you forsaken me?'

8. Delivering himself into the Father's hands in death so that the new age of the outpouring of the Spirit can begin.

The last three psychological phases, the interior states of Jesus' dying, are marked by the 'seven last words', three of compassion, one of abandonment, and three of consigning himself to the Father in a new beginning for the world. The first five steps follow the five stages of dying described by Elizabeth Kübler-Ross in *On Death and Dying*.[2] Dr Kübler-Ross describes how terminally ill patients typically go through five psychological stages as death approaches:

1. denial of the fact that they are dying;
2. anger that this is happening to them;
3. bargaining with the doctor or with God to save them from dying;
4. depression;
5. acceptance of death.

Jesus was like us in everything except sin, so it comes as unsurprising that he suffered through the typical process of those close to death.

Fathers Matthew and Dennis Linn, in their book *Healing Life's Hurts,* pray through Elizabeth Kübler-Ross's five stages of dying 'so that the crippling hurts of life become opportunities for emotional, physical, and spiritual healing'.[3] We can adapt the ideas of the Linn brothers to apply them in a prayer that works through the stages of Jesus' psychological experience, entering into his experience as well as we can, placing our own painful memories and hurtful experiences in his so that by his wounds we may be healed.[4] We will pray through not only the five Kübler-Ross stages, which the Linns have adapted to prayer for inner healing, but also through the three stages of Jesus' dying on the cross.

Each of us has one or more crosses to carry. It might be a cross connected with work; it could be a person or a few people who, willingly or perhaps unwillingly, make life difficult for me; it could be an illness, or a physical or emotional handicap; it could be a pattern of sin that resists being done away with. It could be something I carry from the past: a memory that needs healing; past failure; an unhappy childhood; a loss through death. I can ask the Lord to guide me as to what cross to carry, in prayer, in union with his suffering, so that his wounds may heal mine.

*Taking up the cross and following Jesus in prayer*

'If anyone would come after me, let him deny himself and take up his cross and follow me' (Mark 8.34b). I can deny myself the luxury of self-pity and of any hanging on to resentment or hurt, and I can take up my particular cross, in prayer, with Jesus.

1. Facing reality: Lord Jesus, help me to face my cross squarely. You were completely realistic in facing yours; give me the grace of sharing in that realism. Let me see my cross, my situation, as you see it, through your eyes. I thank you for the growth involved, for the good present, and I ask you to strengthen me to see my own hurt with my eyes open, not denying any of the more painful aspects. (At this point, I can describe the situation to the Lord in my own words, speaking as to a friend who understands perfectly.)

2. Working through resentment and anger: Lord, help me to recognize any anger in myself about this situation. You were not afraid of being angry; help me to recognize and to feel the anger or resentment or sullenness inside me. I unite that anger to the anger that you felt your last time in Jerusalem knowing how it would end. Show me what anger lies in me, and against whom. Show me where I am hurt, and what was and is the reaction in me to that hurt and to what hurt or continues to hurt me. (Describe the hurt and your reaction to it to the Lord, using any emotional language that comes to mind, 'getting out' to him any resentment, anger, hostility, and the roots of any coldness or defensiveness in you.) Take out of my heart, Lord, any anger or resentment that is not from you, that blocks me from forgiving and from loving. I give to you this hostility; take it, Lord; fill me that I may be free to love. Take away

my resentful defensiveness, my hardness of heart, and give me a heart of flesh, a compassionate heart like yours.

3.  Resisting the temptation to bargain: Lord, you accepted your suffering without trying futilely to change those who made you suffer, without making conditions or demanding that things be different. Teach me and help me to be like you, *to accept what I cannot change*, and to carry the cross of what I cannot change in union with you. (Take a moment to look at the Lord and to let him show you whether you are putting conditions on your suffering, such as demanding that other people or the situation be different, and whether you are kicking against the goad. Speak to him in your own words.)

4. Working through sadness and depression: Lord, through your own sadness unto death in your agony in the garden, heal me of all sadness or depression. Help me to recognize any fear in myself and any sadness. Fill me with your love that casts out all fear and sadness and every spirit of depression. By your emotional wounds in the garden of Gethsemane, heal my emotional wounds, and fill the healed places with your love and unconditional acceptance of me just as I am now. (Let the Lord heal you of any depression – which can be anger turned in against yourself, self-hatred – by filling you with his personal love for you. Give him any fear you have, and let him take it away. Tell him how you feel about this cross, and accept his healing power.)

5. Acceptance of the cross: Lord Jesus, I accept this cross, and with you I say to the Father, 'Father, all things are possible to you; remove this cup from me; however, not my will, but yours be done.' Help me to see the possibilities of growth in this cross; you write straight, Lord, with crooked lines; show me the positive side of this cross. I accept it for love of you, in union with you and accepting your compas-

49

sionate love for me. (Tell the Lord that, with his strength, you embrace this cross for him and with him, as your response to his love of you.) Heal me, Lord, so that I can not only accept this cross, but also praise you for everything, including the negative things in my life.

## Praying with Jesus crucified

Paul writes, 'I have been crucified with Christ; it is no longer I who live, but Christ who lives in me' (Gal. 2.20). You can continue to pray about the cross in your life, looking at Jesus on the cross and drawing strength from the healing power of the Crucified. The answer to the song's question, 'Were you there when they crucified my Lord?' is 'I am there now in prayer'.

6. Forgiving: Lord, you can forgive your murderers and pray for them. Forgive me. And give me the power of your forgiveness on the cross so that I can forgive those who have hurt me. I trust in the power to forgive that you have and that you give me. And before you now, I forgive all who have hurt me. (Forgive each person who has knowingly or unknowingly contributed to the cross you are praying about. Tell the Lord that you forgive each one, mentioning the person by name and praying for that person.) Give me, Lord, a compassionate and forgiving heart towards each person who has hurt me.

7. Crying out to the Lord: Lord, I cry out to you. Sometimes I feel alone and abandoned, and you seem far away. Out of the depths I cry to you, Lord. (Do not hesitate truly to lament to the Lord. You might use one of the psalms of lament, such as Psalm 22 or Psalm 69.)

8. Abandonment to the Lord: Lord Jesus Christ, I abandon myself completely to you. With you, I cry out to the Father, 'Father, into your hands I commend my spirit.' And Lord,

like you in your suffering and death, I thirst. I thirst for the power of your spirit. I thirst for healing. I thirst for a new outpouring of your healing Spirit of love on me and on those dear to me. Come, Lord Jesus.

### Praying in other ways for healing through the cross

Christian tradition has developed ways of praying through the suffering and death of Jesus, ways that many find helpful more than ever today, for example, the eucharist, the stations of the cross, devotion to the heart of Jesus, the *Spiritual Exercises* of Ignatius Loyola, and praying through the sorrowful mysteries of the rosary. Unfortunately, these ways of praying sometimes seem to be followed with little faith in the healing power of Jesus and in his loving willingness to heal us. Nevertheless, they remain valuable ways of contemplating the Lord's passion, especially when prayed with faith and trust that in Jesus' suffering and death we find healing and salvation.

The celebration of the eucharist, the way *par excellence* to pray about the Lord's passion and death, commemorates the last supper; since the last supper anticipated the sacrifice of the cross, every eucharist re-presents not only the Lord's supper but also his sacrificial death. The eucharist applies the healing power of the cross of Jesus.[5]

Fathers Matthew and Dennis Linn give valuable suggestions for praying the stations of the cross for the healing of memories, with a prayer outline; they suggest:

One memory of a hurt can be handled in greater depth by watching Christ in each station deal with what I felt when hurt. Thus the memory of being humiliated during seventh grade while giving a wrong answer on TV can be healed as I watch Christ dealing with humiliation in each

51

station. The process is one of giving Christ my feelings and taking on his reactions.[6]

The fourteen stations of the cross (the 'Way of the Cross') can be found along the side walls of most Catholic churches and chapels, but they can be made anywhere, praying through them silently, perhaps using a New Testament account of the passion.[7]

Another part of Christian tradition skips the historical details and goes right to the heart of Jesus' motivation in his passion, his love. In particular, devotion to the heart of Jesus, pierced by the spear, underlines the love of Jesus for each person; the heart symbolizes Jesus' love. Catherine of Siena sums up the Christian life in terms of love and union with Jesus crucified: 'You will find the source of love in the side of Christ crucified, and that is where I wish you to seek your refuge and your abode.'[8] Julian of Norwich, describing her prayer, writes:

He led my understanding to this same wound in his side. And there, within, he showed a fair and delightful place, large enough for all mankind that shall be saved to rest there, in peace and in love. Therewith he brought to my mind the most dear and precious water which he let pour out for love . . . Forthwith this good Lord said most blissfully, 'See, how I have loved you.'[9]

The wisdom of the *Spiritual Exercises* of Ignatius Loyola is the foolishness of the cross, and instructive for all prayer for healing through the cross.[10] Ignatius advises the use of the imagination: 'Imagine Christ our Lord present before you on the cross . . . As I behold Christ in this plight, I shall ponder what presents itself to my mind.'[11] Even more often, he advises bringing the emotions into play. Praying about the passion, we are advised to ask for 'sorrow, compassion, and shame, because the Lord is going to his suffering for my sins',[12] for 'sorrow with Christ in sorrow, anguish with Christ in anguish, tears and deep grief because of the great affliction Christ endures for me'.[13] Notice that these feelings are God's gift, graces of prayer, that we are to ask for. Yet, at the same time, Ignatius counsels us to co-operate with these graces and even to anticipate them, 'to make a great effort . . . to be sad and grieve because of the great sorrow and suffering of Christ the Lord'.[14] And again, 'I will rouse myself to sorrow, suffering, and anguish by frequently calling to mind the labours, fatigue, and suffering which Christ our Lord endured from the time of his birth down to the mystery of the passion upon which I am engaged at present.'[15]

Ignatius focusses not so much on the material aspects of Jesus' suffering as on the interior attitudes. We are asked to contemplate 'what Christ suffers in his human nature', 'what he desires to suffer', 'the most sacred humanity suffering so cruelly', 'that Christ suffers all this for my sins', 'the great fear that overwhelmed him'.[16] Ignatius emphasizes the death of Jesus as 'for my sins' and 'for me'. He stresses Jesus as *my* Saviour. 'I am the meaning of Christ's cross.'[17] It measures his love for me. And Jesus calls me to share in his sufferings, to enter into his experience, to suffer and to anguish with him suffering and in anguish. 'It is only by actually experiencing, with God's grace and in my own way, what he experiences that I will also experience how he has transformed this dying experience into a new creation.'[18] And so through my own dying experience now or in the past, through my own cross, I can be healed into a new creation.

Ignatius also suggests contemplating 'the presence' at the cross 'of his most sorrowful mother', 'her great sorrow and weariness, and also that of the disciples'.[19] This leads to the

53

role of Mary, the mother of Jesus, in praying for healing through the cross.

## Jesus' mother at the cross

Luke's gospel understands Mary as a model for the Christian and also as a figure of the faithful remnant of Israel, of the 'poor' who remain faithful to God through suffering (Luke 1.48,52; Zeph. 2.3; 3.12-15). He includes her in Jesus' redemptive suffering. Simeon prophesies: 'This child is set . . . for a sign that is spoken against (and a sword will pierce through your own heart also)' (Luke 2.34b-35a). But it is John's gospel that describes Mary's place at the foot of the cross.

For John, Mary is principally a model of faith. Her faith at the cross continues the faith she shows at the wedding party of Cana (John 2.1-12). John's gospel puts Cana and the cross in parallel. They mark the beginning and the end of Jesus' public ministry; in both, Mary, present, is referred to as Jesus' mother, and called by Jesus 'woman'; and both texts refer to a providential 'hour'. John clearly intends these three parallels to symbolize deeper realities.

At Cana, Mary asks Jesus to work a miracle in order to save the situation, embarrassing for the hosts, of running out of wine. At her asking, he does it. In keeping with the spirit of John's gospel, I can ask Mary to do what she did at Cana: ask Jesus to save the situation. I can ask anyone to pray for me or with me or both; so too, with greater reason because of the precedent of Cana, can I ask Jesus' mother to pray with me and for me for the inner healing that comes from the power of Jesus' cross.[20] She is his mother, and she was there at his death.

Praying for inner healing, I can cry out to God with her, lamenting with her.[21] I can join my lament to her sorrow at the foot of the cross, joining my hurts to hers. I can pray to the Father, with Jesus' mother:

> Times and seasons change,
> centuries and ages pass;
> you seem above them, Lord,
> untouched, unmoved.
>
> But
> your son entered in,
> born of a woman,
> crushed and crucified,
> to ransom us.
>
> Will you be deaf to our cries?
> Can you ignore the appeals
> of the creatures your Son embraced?
> Can you refuse the prayer
> of Mary, his mother?
>
> Let us know the freedom of your kingdom
> where you live with your Son
> and with the Holy Spirit,
> one infinite freedom,
> for ever and ever. Amen.[22]

# 5

# *Being Healed through Praise and the Gifts of the Spirit*

The first words of the prologue to Ignatius Loyola's *Spiritual Exercises* are: 'Man was created to praise.' This echoes Paul's Letter to the Ephesians 1.5-6: 'He destined us in love to be his sons through Jesus Christ, according to the purpose of his will, to the praise of his glorious grace which he freely bestowed on us in the Beloved.' Created to praise God as one of our most important activities, we can expect the Lord to make us more whole, more human, more integrated, through doing something for which he made us: praising him. Praise heals. Rather, when we praise him, he heals us through our praise.

### *Praise*

What do I mean by praise? For one thing, praise differs from thanksgiving. When I thank God, I show him gratitude for his gifts and, in my prayer, I refer those gifts back to him in my thanks. But when I praise God, I give him credit, so to speak, not for his gifts but simply for himself. 'Praise is the point at which thanksgiving becomes thanking God for being God, or in the words of the *Gloria*, "We give you thanks for your great glory." '[1] I can praise God for his actions, for the things he does, or I can praise him for his creation, or for any part of his creation; I can praise the Lord

56

for anything and for everything, because he is the Lord of all things. Or I can just praise him for himself and for his qualities: his goodness, his love, his wisdom, his infinite greatness. I am not thanking him, precisely; rather, I praise him for being the kind of Lord he is, and for being the kind of Lord he is to have done these things, to have created these things to exist in this way, to act as he acts.

Praise is something like adoration, but more active, more going-out to God, speaking interiorly or out loud, or shouting, or singing, or dancing. Praise celebrates God. Adoration connotes the quiet or silent prostration of one's whole self before God (Rev. 4.10; 7.11). Praise has voice:

> They cried 'Amen! Alleluia!' Then a voice came from the throne; it said: 'Praise our God, all you his servants, you who fear him, small and great.' Then I heard what seemed to be the voice of a great multitude, like the sound of mighty thunderpeals, crying, 'Alleluia! For the Lord our God the Almighty reigns' (Rev. 19.4b-6).

Praise gives nothing to God; it simply acclaims him, applauds him, for who he is. Praise acclaims the Lord now – for what he has done, or does, or has always been and is. But praise does not look to the past nor even to the future; it looks straight at the Lord and claps its hands.

Praise means giving glory to God, glorifying him through praise of his revealed glory. And so the First Vatican Council (1869-1870) declares that 'the world was made for the glory of God'.[2] This 'glory of God' includes both the glory that God gives to his creatures and through which they manifest his greatness, and also the praise that we should give God as a response to the manifestations of his greatness. Nature and history show forth God's glory. 'The world is charged with the grandeur of God; it will flame out like shining from shook foil' (G. M. Hopkins, 'God's Gran-

57

deur'). And we are called to lift up praise to God, to glorify him in response to his glory that he reveals to us. Following Saint Paul, who writes that we are appointed and destined to live for the praise of the glory of the Lord (Eph. 1.12,14), Elizabeth of the Trinity wanted to be nothing other than 'a praise of glory'.[3] 'Glory be to God,' Hopkins writes, 'praise him' ('Pied Beauty').

'Praise names', lists of laudatory titles recited to the king or to other illustrious personages, form the most important part of Bantu oral literature. Christian litanies are a kind of 'praise names' to the Lord, and include prayer of supplication ('pray for us' or 'free us, Lord,' or 'we beg you, hear us,' for example). The litany of the Holy Name of Jesus, the litanies of the Sacred Heart and of the Precious Blood of Jesus, and the litany of Loreto are good examples. The titles, the invocations – which vary, like 'praise names' – are praise; the supplications, constant, complement them.

Many of the psalms are prayers or hymns of praise. They have a simple structure. A brief introduction sets the tone of praise: 'Praise the Lord! Praise the Lord, O my soul!' (Psalm 146); 'I will extol you, my God and King, and bless your name for ever and ever' (Psalm 145); 'Praise the Lord, all nations' (Psalm 117); 'Make a joyful noise to the Lord, all the lands!' (Psalm 100); 'Bless the Lord, O my soul' (Psalms 103 and 104). There follows the content of the praise, what the psalm praises God for: his creation (e. g. Psalms 104 and 148); his goodness to us (e. g. Psalms 103, 117 and 145); his mighty deeds (e. g. Psalms 29 and 113). The conclusion repeats the opening shout of praise, such as 'Praise the Lord,' or 'O Lord, our Lord, how majestic is your name in all the earth' (Psalm 8), or it sums up the main themes of praise in the body of the psalm: 'For the Lord is good, his steadfast love endures for ever, and his faithfulness to all generations' (Psalm 100).

Other psalms of praise are scattered throughout the Old Testament. These include Isaiah 25, which begins, 'O Lord, you are my God; I will exalt you; I will praise your name'; Isaiah 42.10-13, 'Sing to the Lord a new song, his praise from the end of the earth!', and Nahum 1.2-8, which praises God for being 'a jealous God and avenging' (v. 2). Moses' song of God's victory, 'I will sing to the Lord, for he has triumphed gloriously, the horse and his rider he has thrown into the sea' (Exod. 15.1-18), praises the Lord for saving his people from the Pharaoh's troops, for his power, and for his steadfast love. And praise is frequent in the historical books; Jehoshaphat appoints those who are to sing to the Lord and praise him in holy array, as they went before the army, and say, 'Give thanks to the Lord, for his steadfast love endures for ever' (II Chron. 20.21).

In the New Testament, Luke's gospel and the Acts of the Apostles give an important place to praise. In the gospel, the praise begins with Mary's *Magnificat* (Luke 1.46-55), the song of Zechariah (Luke 1.68-79), and with the angels (Luke 2.13-14) and the shepherds (Luke 2.20) praising and glorifying God at the birth of Jesus. It continues with Simeon, who blesses God and praises him in a brief hymn (2.28-32) and the prophetess Anna (2.38). Luke frequently shows those whom Jesus heals glorifying and praising God, as well as those who witness Jesus' healings and other miracles.[4] The blind man of Jericho, for example, his sight restored, glorifies God 'and all the people, when they saw it, gave praise to God' (18.43). In Acts, the Christian community (2.47), the man healed at the gate called Beautiful (3.8-9), converts (10.46; 13.48; 19.17), and all present (4.21; 11.18; 19.17; 21.20) praise and glorify God.

The letters of Paul often begin with praise, especially the letters to the Ephesians and the Colossians, and the two letters to Timothy contain bursts of praise. The Book of

Revelation frequently refers to singing God's praises. The four living creatures sing, 'Holy, holy, holy is the Lord God Almighty' (4.8); the twenty-four elders praise God singing (4.10-11) and praying (11.16-17), and together they say, 'Amen, Alleluia!' (19.4).[5]

Christian worship has always emphasized praise, not only in hymns and in the divine office, but especially in the celebration of the Lord's supper; the eucharistic liturgies, universally, are prayers of praise as well as of petition and thanksgiving.

### Praise and personal integration

By praising the Lord, I open my heart to him. I take a stance of worship, going out to God on his own terms, not for what he does for me personally, but for who he is. And in opening myself to the Lord through praise, I open the door of my heart to his healing grace and to all his gifts; I become especially receptive to his Holy Spirit, who praises Jesus and the Father in me and through me, and in whom I offer praise to God.

Saint Augustine writes that praise does not help the Lord, adds nothing to him; but praise does aid us, serve us, help us to grow.[6] 'Not that God grows through our praises, but that we do.'[7] We grow in that, doing what we were created for and turning ourselves entirely to the Lord to whom we are headed, we become more ourselves, more what the Lord has destined us to be from the beginning; that is, closer to him, more integrated as persons, more healed.

The use, in praising God, of the gift of tongues provides us with probably the best example of the Lord's use of our own praise to heal us interiorly.[8] The gift of tongues has, as purpose, prayer of petition, but also and predominantly, praise; it is chiefly a gift of praise. Studies have shown that speaking in tongues, ordinarily at least, does not have the structure of a real language. It is a kind of babbling to God, a sort of pre-speech like that of an infant who cannot yet speak but who makes non-sensical sounds. Praying in tongues is non-conceptual vocal prayer, somewhat analogous to just being silently and without concepts before the Lord. The sounds made are often repetitive, and we can compare praying in tongues in some ways with saying the rosary or any similar repetitive prayer. The principal use of the gift of tongues is for personal prayer, although a communal use is often found in prayer groups that praise God together speaking or singing in tongues. When Paul writes to the Corinthians to limit the use of the gift of tongues in their prayer assemblies, he refers to *prophesying* in tongues, a different use of the gift from that of praying in tongues (I Cor. 14.26-33). Because of the very non-conceptual nature of speaking in tongues, if used in prophecy in a group, an inspired interpretation should follow; and again because of its non-conceptual nature, tongue-speaking's main function is quietly praising the Lord in personal prayer. So Paul tells the Corinthians that, if there is no one present to interpret prophecies in tongues, then let each 'keep silent in church and speak to himself and to God' (I Cor. 14.28).

Praise tends to shift and change the use of words. Language breaks down under praise's weight. The aim of praise is not to communicate messages, so the language of praise usually omits the verbs and strings out titles in succession – 'Lamb of God, Lord God, God Almighty' – like Bantu praise names, like litanies. Praise tends to manifest an attitude, a way of beholding the one praised, rather than to communicate precise meanings. And concepts, often, cannot hold the content of praise; words fail. Where praise transcends concepts, the gift of tongues begins. According to Saint Paul, praying in tongues builds up the one who prays, even

61

though that person does not understand what he says in his prayer; because, while his spirit prays, his understanding rests (I Cor. 14.14).

The gift of tongues is not a kind of ecstatic speech or utterance from a trance-like state, nor does it belong exclusively to any particular Christian group or groups. Peter Hocken has expressed it well:

Much misunderstanding and confusion stem from the focus on the language-aspect (any prayer of praise may not be linguistically impressive!) and from treating this phenomenon as 'extraordinary' . . . From the nature of the case, anyone whose prayer has become predominantly the prayer of praise is near to praying in tongues; and it is really as simple as asking God for the extra push and letting it come . . . Of its nature [praying in tongues] requires a letting go of our self-control, of our tight grip on ourselves. It is within prayer a form of dying to self and rising to new life . . .[9]

I have met several people who have no contact with Pentecostal churches nor with any kind of charismatic groups, but who have the gift of tongues and who use it in their private prayer. It is not an unusual gift; on the contrary. The point should be made, however, that it is a gift, and that it is principally a gift of praise. The gift is not to make incomprehensible sounds, but that the sounds be prayer. To coin an image in a mangled metaphor, praise in tongues looks at the Lord and claps its vocal chords.

Sometimes the sentence of Saint Paul, 'We do not know how to pray as we ought, but the Spirit himself intercedes for us with sighs too deep for words' (Rom. 8.26), is applied to prayer in tongues. However, the Holy Spirit obviously does not take the place of the person or of the interior spirit of the person praying. Rather, 'the Spirit himself together with our spirit' (Rom. 8.16) praises God. Prayer in tongues is a rational act, even though under the influence of grace and having a non-conceptual content. It is a praying 'in the Spirit'.

The content of prayer in tongues seems to come from unconscious or preconscious areas of the psyche, from regions of ourselves at the centre of our persons but below the level of consciousness. Perhaps for this reason, praying in tongues has an intensely personal quality, expresses somehow the uniqueness of the person praying. Although not structured like ordinary languages, praying in tongues contains the essence of language: not primarily the communication of ideas, but the expression to another (in this case to God) of the person speaking. Praying in tongues is a language the way that music, painting and dancing are languages; it is praise as self-expression, the very self as praise, the beginning of 'the new name which no one knows except him who receives it' (Rev. 2.17). Each gift of tongues is a personal and personalized language of prayer.

Again perhaps partly because the content of prayer in tongues seems to come from the below-consciousness levels of the one praying, the use of the gift has an integrating effect, heals the person praying gradually over a long period of habitual use of the gift. In praying in tongues, the whole person – conscious and infraconscious, physical and emotional and spiritual, social and private – prays, and so a synthesis-in-action takes place, unifying all the strands and parts and fragments of the one who prays. The understanding, the intelligence, rests, subsumed into the whole of the person; western cultures tend to isolate intelligence and to cut it off from intuition so that it hardens into rigidity. In prayer in tongues, the understanding takes a vacation and gains new strength from the rest of the person. And the person gains a new spontaneity of expression and of existence. Praying in tongues unifies and integrates, and so heals interiorly, the person who uses it.

Morton T. Kelsey writes that,

> . . . in many of the cases which have been observed tongues appears to be associated with growth and integration of personality . . . Tongue speakers make it clear that there is an emotional release. One finds that it is easier to express emotions and to give way to them in a creative way. There is also a sense of joy even in the midst of difficulties . . . Speaking with tongues is one evidence of the Spirit of God working in the unconscious and bringing one to a new wholeness, a new integration of the total psyche, a process which the Church has traditionally called sanctification.[10]

## The healing gifts of the Spirit

All the gifts of the Spirit heal us, in different ways. The Holy Spirit himself is the gift of Jesus and the Father, and his presence heals us.

The Father loves Jesus, and Jesus loves the Father; this mutual love between Jesus and the Father relates them to one another with a divine force that has its own personal identity. The relationship of mutual love between the Father and Jesus subsists as their Holy Spirit. The Father and Jesus relate us to themselves by sending us their Spirit; they catch us up into the life of the Trinity, into the divine community, by making us share in that which unites them in mutual love. In John's gospel, Jesus speaks of himself and the Father as 'we': 'The Father and I are one' (John 10.30); 'We are one' (John 17.22). This 'Divine We' extends to us: 'All should be one as you, Father, in me, and I in you; all should be one in us' (John 17.21). 'If someone loves me, he will keep my word and my Father will love him' (John 14.23). Sharing in the 'Divine We' of Jesus and the Father through their Spirit in our hearts, we become more *'we'*, more one, more united. The 'Divine We' as such is the Holy Spirit, who relates the Father and Jesus, and us to them and to one another.[11] The Holy Spirit is given to us by Jesus and the Father; he is Gift; and he is the Love who unites us to Jesus, to the Father, to each other, leading us to holiness.[12]

This means that every deepening of the relationship between Jesus and the person united to him involves a new sending of the Holy Spirit, a deepening of the Spirit's indwelling in that person's heart; we exist in a new way, closer to Jesus and to the Father in the Spirit. This new way of existing is what we call grace.[13]

The Holy Spirit manifests himself in our experience; we experience what he does in us. In Luke's gospel and in the Acts of the Apostles, the Spirit is the divine power. The angel says to Mary: 'The Holy Spirit will come upon you; the power of the Most High will overshadow you' (Luke 2.35). In this typical Hebrew parallelism, 'Holy Spirit' and 'power of the Most High' parallel and reinforce each other; they mean the same. The Holy Spirit *is* power. In the Acts of the Apostles, Jesus tells his apostles, 'You shall receive power when the Holy Spirit has come upon you' (Acts 1.8). In John's gospel, the Spirit, the Paraclete, comforts, consoles and strengthens us;[14] the Spirit *speaks* to us, shows us the meaning of God's word, and prompts us to witness to the words of Jesus.[15] In Paul's letters, the Holy Spirit *works* in us; he prays in us, he frees us (Rom. 8.2, 26). He makes Jesus dwell in us (Rom 8.9-10; II Cor. 3.18; Gal. 2.20). He gives us the power to say, 'Jesus is Lord', and he manifests himself through his various gifts (II Cor. 12.3-4). All these operations of the Spirit in us speak of our experiencing the Holy Spirit. For this reason, the traditional formulations of what the Holy Spirit does in us have been in terms of experience. The Holy Spirit gives us his gifts: wisdom, understanding, counsel, fortitude, piety, knowledge, fear of the Lord (see Isa. 11.2-3). We experience the fruits of the Spirit in us: love, joy, peace, patience, kindness, goodness, faithfulness, gentleness, self-control (Gal. 5.22-23).

These lists of what the Spirit does in all in whom he lives do not of course define completely what he does in us; they describe in an incomplete way the Spirit's activities in every Christian. We can call these the common gifts of the Spirit. Besides these gifts common to all to whom Jesus sends his Spirit, the Spirit gives special gifts, charisms. Charisms are given to some, but not to all; however, the Body of Christ possesses all the charisms even though no one member has them all. Saint Paul lists charisms in various places in his writings, and of course none of these lists, nor even all of them taken together, exhausts the variety and diversity of charisms that the Spirit bestows. The classic list of charisms, in I Corinthians 12, names as charisms 'the utterance of wisdom, the utterance of knowledge, faith, gifts of healing, the working of miracles, prophecy, discernment of spirits, and various kinds of tongues and their interpretation' (I Cor. 12.8-10). In other places, Paul also lists as charisms: teaching, helping, evangelizing, administrating, leading, serving, exhorting, and alms-giving.[16] The Second Vatican Council, in its Decree on the Missions, names the missionary vocation as a charism.[17] Evangelical poverty has long been understood as a charism, especially since the great outpouring of the charism of poverty in the early Middle Ages with Saint Francis of Assisi and others. In the Jesuit tradition, the gift of tears has always been considered a charism. And every religious order has its own particular charism or cluster of charisms as exemplified in its founders and in its greatest members.

A charism is both a call from God and the means to respond to that call. A particular charism enables a person to respond to the Holy Spirit in a special way, to receive the Spirit's action in a particular way. It makes the person a channel of the Holy Spirit in some special mode: according to leadership, or prayer, or mission, or healing, or governing, or something else. A charism makes the Spirit 'visible', as it were, or 'tangible' in the Christian community. A charism is a gift for service, for the building up of the Body of Christ. But because the gift comes from God, a charism is primarily a new way of relating to God, a new way of being in Jesus.

Every charism, of course, is a gift; we have no right to any gift from the Lord. On the other hand, we do have the right and also the obligation to ask for the gifts that we need to be more healed. I have known missionaries who suffered from what I can describe only as an insufficiency of the charism of being a missionary. Those in positions of religious leadership can and should pray for new outpourings of the charism of leadership. Many persons who have answered the Lord's call to them to belong to him in a life of consecrated celibacy have prayed for an increase in the charism of consecrated celibacy (Matt. 19.12; I Cor. 7.7) and been healed in their emotions, in their total affectivity. There are, surely, special gifts of being a good Christian father, mother, husband, wife; where needed, they can be prayed for. The Lord hears us when we cry out, and he answers. When we cry out for gifts that we need to be healed, he gives them.

And sometimes the Lord does not wait for us to ask, but takes advantage of our openness to him in praising him, and gifts us with healing. Alleluia (which means, 'Praise the Lord')!

# 6

## *Jesus is Lord*

In the gospels of Mark, Matthew and Luke, the Kingdom occupies a central place in the teaching of Jesus; it is one of his main themes. In the Acts of Apostles and, especially, in the Pauline writings, the theme of the Kingdom becomes the theme of the Lordship of Jesus. I would like to describe the New Testament concept of Jesus' Lordship, then to comment on the importance of this concept for prayer for inner healing, and finally to reflect on the meaning of Jesus' Lordship for hope in the future.

### *The Lordship of Jesus in the New Testament*

The key to the whole idea of Christ's Lordship is Jesus' use of Psalm 110.[1] This stands behind the early church's understanding that Jesus is Lord, and, surely, somehow lies at the origin of the concept.[2] The application of the title 'Lord' to Jesus occurs rarely in the synoptic gospels with the exception of Luke, who uses it eighteen times. It is not a title that Jesus applies to himself during his public ministry, and – as Acts and the Pauline writings show clearly – the primitive Christian community understood Jesus to be constituted Lord by his passion, death, and resurrection. It is, then, to Jesus' use of Psalm 110 that one must look. The context is that of public exchange with the Pharisees (Matt. 22.41-46) and the scribes (Mark 12.35-37; Luke 20.41-44).

And as Jesus taught in the temple, he said, 'How can the scribes say that the Christ is the son of David? David himself, inspired by the Holy Spirit, declared, ''The Lord said to my Lord, sit at my right hand till I put your enemies under your feet.'' David himself calls him Lord, so how is he his son?' And the great throng heard him gladly (Mark 12.35-37).

Psalm 110 is referred to again in the synoptic gospels in conjunction with a reference to the messianic passage of Daniel 7.14 (Matt. 26.64; Mark 14.61; Luke 22.69), in the confrontation of Jesus and the high priest.

Again the high priest asked him, 'Are you the Christ, the Son of the Blessed?' And Jesus said, 'I am; and you will see the Son of man seated at the right hand of Power, and coming with the clouds of heaven' (Mark 14.60-61).

Jesus identifies himself with Daniel 7.14's Son of man figure who comes with the clouds of heaven. But the phrase 'seated at the right hand of power' is from Psalm 110: 'Sit at my right hand'. Here, having already entered into the paschal mystery, in his passion, Jesus identifies himself, by his use of Psalm 110, with the 'Lord' to whom the Lord speaks in verse 1. The whole passion story itself, with a kind of sublime and mysterious irony that one can hardly grasp, speaks of Jesus as King and Lord particularly in the passages concerning his being mocked, his conversation with Pilate, his presentation by Pilate to the people ('*ecce homo*', and the inscription on the cross 'King of the Jews').

How did the learned people of Jesus' time understand Psalm 110? Something can be gleaned from early Jewish literature on Psalm 110; even though the Talmuds and the Midrash were compiled much later than the time of Christ, they reflect opinions handed down from earlier periods. There is nothing in the Jerusalem Talmud, but the more important Babylonian Talmud contains two significant mentions of Psalm 110, identifying the (second) 'lord' with Abraham. However, the Midrash on Psalm 110, also equating Abraham and the 'lord', points out that verse 1 of Psalm 110 is, at the same time, a messianic text. At any rate, Jesus' messianic use of the text tells us that it was considered, at least by some at that time, to be messianic. We can only speculate on Jesus' own study of Psalm 110 as 'he grew in age and grace and wisdom', and of his use of it in his explanation of the scriptures to the two disciples on the road to Emmaus.

The early church's use of the title 'Lord' for Jesus refers to the risen and glorified Jesus, with a certain emphasis on his divinity (he is at the right hand of the Father). The word 'lord', *kyrios*, is the word for God in the Septuagint Greek of the Old Testament; in most English translations of the Old Testament it is rendered as 'Lord'. Using the same title for Jesus, of course, is to say he is equal to God the Father.

Already part of the basic kerygma of the church in its first beginnings, Psalm 110 finds use in the Pentecost discourse of Peter (Acts 2.34-36), who concludes, 'Let all the house of Israel therefore know assuredly that God has made him both Lord and Christ, this Jesus whom you crucified.' Stephen, at his death by stoning, gazes upward and sees 'the Son of man standing at the right hand of God' (Acts 7.56). And, further, some evidence shows that the mysterious 'baptism in the name of Jesus' refers to the liturgical practice that had the person baptized say, during the rite, 'Jesus is Lord'.

In any case, the phrase 'Jesus is Lord' is one of the oldest in the Pauline writings. It occurs six times (Phil. 2.11; I Cor. 8.6 and 12.3; II Cor. 4.5; Rom. 10.9; Col. 2.6), and certainly antedates all the letters. Add to this the phrase, *marana tha* ('come, Lord') or *maran atha* ('the Lord is coming') of

70

I Corinthians 16.22, a phrase which is repeated in the Book of Revelation (22.20b).

Perhaps most interesting is the passage of the Letter to the Philippians 2.5-11, which is so much commented on:

Have this mind among yourselves which is yours in Christ Jesus, who, though he was in the form of God, did not count equality with God a thing to be grasped, but emptied himself, taking the form of a servant, being born in the likeness of men. And being found in human form he humbled himself and became obedient unto death, even death on a cross. Therefore God has highly exalted him and bestowed on him the name which is above every name, that at the name of Jesus every knee should bow, in heaven and on earth, and every tongue confess that Jesus Christ is Lord, to the glory of God the Father.

'The name which is above every name' is the title 'Lord', given to Jesus as the divine response to his suffering and death, to his 'emptying out' of himself, his *kenosis*, which begins with his incarnation and reaches a high (or, rather, low) point in his death on a cross. The contrast between 'the form of God' and 'human form' is meant to be striking. The stress is on Jesus' humility and obedience ('even unto death') to the Father. In the final point of his *kenosis*, his death, Jesus descends into the heart of the world so that, in his resurrection, he can be the heart of the world, Lord in a true and even ontological way – not simply appointed or named juridically, but Lord in such a way that to uproot him would be to make the world cease to exist.

The same doctrine of Jesus' universal and organic (as opposed to merely juridical) Lordship is contained in the first three chapters of the Letter to the Ephesians. 'He [the Father] has put all things under his [Jesus'] feet, and made him, as the ruler of everything, the head of the church –

which is his body, and the fullness of him who fills the whole creation' (Eph 1.22).

The Letter to the Colossians (1.13–2.15), and especially what appears to be a previously existing hymn (1.15-20), views the whole universe as somehow suspended from Christ, anchored in him: 'in him all things hold together' (v. 17); 'for in him all the fullness of God was pleased to dwell, and through him to reconcile to himself all things' (vv. 19-20); the image differs from that of the Letter to the Ephesians, where Christ is seen as filling the universe. Here, in the Letter to the Colossians, the image is the opposite – of all things being (reconciled to God) in Christ; but the doctrine is the same: the universal Lordship of Jesus.

Because all creation comes under Jesus' Lordship, all of creation shares in God's plan of salvation.

> Creation still retains the hope of being freed, like us, from its slavery to decadence, to enjoy the same freedom and glory as the children of God. From the beginning till now the entire creation, as we know, has been groaning in one great act of giving birth (Rom. 8.21-22).

The world is related to Christ through people in such a way that the world itself is an object of salvation, of redemption, of final transformation. Jesus, through us, is the hope of the world and the guarantee to us of the meaningfulness of the world. He is the Father's promise that something permanent of what we make, suffer, work through the world, will endure.

Furthermore, Jesus is the centre of the Father's plan for the world. God's plan, which has been revealed to us in Jesus, is that all things on earth and in heaven be brought together under Jesus as head, that all things be recapitulated in Jesus. God has planned from the beginning of time that all things that exist be reconciled, unified, harmonized, in

Jesus. This divine plan underlies human history and gives it its deepest meaning.

The Second Vatican Council, in 'The Pastoral Constitution on the Church in the Modern World' *(Gaudium et Spes)*, understands the whole world and all of history as centred on the risen Lord. He is the goal of human history, the future focal point of all true progress. At its best and most profound level, human history is moving toward the ultimate reconciliation of all things in Jesus.[3]

Jesus is not only the goal of the world's movement into the future; he is actively present in all of history and in the whole universe. The fullness of the risen Jesus' active presence and influence is in the church; but, at the same time, his presence fills the whole creation (Eph. 1.22-23), which holds together in him (Col. 1.17) in such a way that everything depends on him and finds its meaning and its value and even its existence in Jesus risen.

The Letter to the Hebrews (1.13) quotes Psalm 110 at the end of a series of 'proof texts' to show the Lordship of Jesus (see also 8.1 and 10.12-13). And it goes further than the other Pauline writings in its use of Psalm 110, taking up the idea of the priesthood according to Melchisedek (Psalm 110.4; Heb. 6.20–7.20), thus associating Jesus' priesthood with his Lordship. The idea is that Jesus is not only Lord in his own right, but he sits at the Father's right hand as eternal high priest to intercede for us. He is our priest, our mediator, with the Father.

### The Lordship of Jesus in Christian life

Besides recognizing Jesus' Lordship over everything, we are called to recognize Jesus as our own personal Lord. Just as the Lord Jesus gives meaning and existence to the whole world, so he gives me my personal meaning and existence.

Just as all history finds its true meaning and its fulfilment in Jesus, so I find my own true meaning and fulfilment in him. Jesus risen is present in all of history and in the whole universe, and he is actively present in my whole personal history and in every part of my life. I find my personal value, meaning, existence, and fulfilment in the risen Jesus. And just as the Father's plan from the beginning of time has been to recapitulate all things in Christ, to unify and reconcile everything in Jesus, so, too, the Father's plan is and always has been to unify and to reconcile everything in my being and in my life in Jesus, to integrate me, to give me personal unity, to knit up the frazzled parts of myself, in and through and under the Lordship of Jesus.

Jesus calls me not only to accept his love and his Lordship, but to participate actively in the Father's plan to recapitulate all things in himself. Jesus invites me to bring everything in my life under his Lordship: my worries, my problems, my anxieties and fears, my failures, my successes, my hopes for myself and for others, everything. I can take each preoccupation, every burden, all difficulties and sorrows and joys to Jesus, placing them in his hands, under his loving Lordship.

To the extent that I do, I will be co-operating with the Lord in his becoming the Lord of my whole life in a conscious way on my part. My prayer and my other activities will become more and more integrated so that my whole life becomes a prayer. My life will cease to be torn in two directions between an 'upward' component of faith in God, of worship and love of God, and a 'forward' component of faith in other persons, in my work, in the whole human enterprise in general and in my particular part in that enterprise. I will stop being torn between the 'upward' and the 'forward'. The Lord will heal me, make me whole, make an integration in me, a synthesis of all the elements and aspects of my life; he does this with my co-operation by which I bring everything in my life, consciously and explicitly, prayerfully, under his Lordship in conscious recognition of his Lordship over everything.

Distractions in prayer play an important role in Christian life. They show me where healing is needed in my life. I am not referring so much to minor distractions like a fly buzzing as to preoccupations. I can be praying and find my mind on another matter, on work to be done, on my brother who is seriously ill, on someone who has hurt me, on a problem coming up. This kind of distraction indicates what is on my mind that is not integrated into my personal relationship with Jesus Christ. It shows up what is not under his Lordship, what I have not yet consciously and fully brought into the zone of the power of his love for me. If it is a distraction, falling outside my relationship with the Lord in prayer, then it is – in my life as a whole – not yet in his hands. In my prayer, I can put the matter into his hands, turning the distraction into a prayer. In this way, I co-operate with him in his work of reconciling the various things on my mind by bringing them into a unity in him; I let him integrate me, pull me together, become more the centre of my life.

If I have a poor relationship with someone, I can put it in the Lord's hands, praying for that person and asking the Lord to heal the relationship and to fill it with his love. If I am distracted by the thought of someone I love, I can bring that person and that relationship to the Lord in my prayer, praying for the person and letting the Lord fill the relationship with his grace and his love, healing any selfishness or possessiveness in me and straightening out the relationship. Distractions are clues as to what I should put prayerfully and explicitly under Jesus' Lordship for healing. Risen, he carries, glorified, the wounds of his passion; it is through those glorified wounds that I am healed.

My recognition of Jesus' Lordship is, itself, a gift: 'No one can say "Jesus is Lord" unless he is under the influence of the Holy Spirit' (I Cor. 12.3). It is not so much that I claim him as my Lord as that I let *him* claim *me*. I give up being lord of my own life, letting go and entering, with my whole life, freely and consciously into the realm of his Lordship by willingly accepting that Lordship.

When people say that 'Jesus is Lord', that is what they are talking about. They are celebrating his resurrection and his victory over the world, they are affirming his Lordship over the whole of creation, and they are putting their whole selves under his Lordship, allowing him to be their Lord.

## Theological reflection

How can we think of the Lordship of Jesus in such a way as to integrate into one meaning the two ideas that Jesus is my personal Lord, and Jesus is the universal Lord of everything? I would like to line up some thoughts in the direction of such an integration. The idea is to see how the *universal* Lordship of Jesus has meaning at the *personal* level.

The Father's revealed word to us is, in the first instance, Jesus himself, risen and glorified. The totality of divine revelation is contained in the risen Jesus, and only in him. But Jesus, in his present glorified state, belongs – in some mysterious way – to the end of the world, as he who is to come. His resurrection happened as historical fact; but the resurrection event has one foot in history (the empty tomb) and one foot in the ages to come, in the New Jerusalem that Jesus inaugurates with his resurrection. That is, Jesus' own resurrection anticipates the final transformation at the end of history, and it somehow belongs, as the beginning, to that final transformation that marks the end-point of history.

We will not fully understand the Father's word to us in Jesus until history has reached its terminal point at Jesus' final coming. Although divine revelation is complete in Jesus risen, it will not be complete for us until history is over. This is true, also, because history itself reveals God and his plan; so revelation, as far as our understanding of it is concerned, will not be complete until history is completed.

Therefore, the full meaning of history will be revealed only at the end of time. The full meaning of anything, then, will not be seen until history's end. Further, the essence of anything is determined only by what it finally becomes. The essential identity of a person can be determined only by what that person ultimately becomes; this is part of the meaning of the parable of the workers who arrive at the eleventh hour (Matt. 20.1-16) and of the conversion of the good thief on Calvary (Luke 23.40-43). Everything and every person is oriented toward its final consummation and fulfilment in the risen Jesus. Every creature finds its true meaning and direction in Jesus. This orientation of all things to Jesus is what we mean when we say Jesus is Lord.

The essence of anything, and the identity of any person, is a function of that person's relation to Jesus – because he is the final judge who assigns to each its final post, its final meaning, and who will illuminate its entire existence utterly. So we are not yet what God has destined us to be from the beginning; we do not yet possess our true identities. Each of us is becoming, is in process toward his true self. We are becoming ourselves, and this becoming is a relationship with Jesus. In the Book of Revelation, the Lord tells us that at the end of this life, at the end of the personal history of each one, he will give to each person 'a white stone, with a new name written on the stone which no one knows except him who receives it' (2.17). This new name is

77

the person's true identity, hidden now in the risen Jesus.

I, too, will be truly myself only when I am at last with the risen Jesus; and only then will I really be and know who I am. My authentic existence is in him, and the meaning of my life is hidden in him.

This is what is meant by creation in Christ. All creation, and every creature, is relative to Jesus, and finds its true self by going out of itself toward him, by leaving itself to find itself in Jesus Christ (Matt. 10.39; Mark 8.35; Luke 9.24; John 12.25). God's creative act, that holds the world and each thing in it in existence, and that moves the world and each part forward (and this is history), is mediated through the risen Jesus. It is only in its relation to him that things exist (John 1.1-4; Col. 1.16-17). And this mediation of the existence and the meaning and the fulfilment of everything is what we mean by the Lordship of Jesus. This is what we say when we say 'Jesus is Lord'.

We see here the relationship between hope and personal prayerful relationship with Jesus. Jesus' resurrection, although a historical fact, belongs by its nature to the end of this world and to the world to come. It anticipates and inaugurates the next world. Furthermore, by reason of his risen state, Jesus transcends all space and time; he is present by his power and Lordship and active influence everywhere and always. Because he anticipates the ultimate future and all that leads to it, he contains that future – and the entire future – in an anticipatory way in himself. The future is, inchoatively, in Jesus. He holds the future in his hands, the future of the world and the personal future of everyone. For the Christian, Jesus Christ is the future.

And, present for me and holding my future in himself, he makes my future – hidden in him – present. In this way he is the ground of my hope. I can hope in the future because, even though I do not know what the future holds, I know who holds the future – Jesus Christ, who stands as the Father's promise to me of an ultimately successful outcome of my life, and who heals me of all fear of the future by filling me with hope in him.

*Marana tha*. Come, Lord Jesus.

# Notes

## Chapter One

1. On healing in general, see especially: Francis MacNutt, *Healing*, Notre Dame: Ave Maria 1974, and *Power to Heal*, Notre Dame: Ave Maria 1977; Barbara Shlemon, *Healing Prayer*, Notre Dame: Ave Maria 1976; Agnes Sanford, *The Healing Light*, Plainfield NY: Logos 1947; Morton Kelsey, *Healing and Christianity*, New York: Harper and London: SCM Press 1973.

2. On inner healing specifically, see especially: Matthew and Dennis Linn, *Healing of Memories: Prayer and Confession – Steps to Inner Healing*, New York: Paulist 1974, and *Healing Life's Hurts*, New York: Paulist 1978; Ruth Stapleton, *The Gift of Inner Healing*, Waco: Word 1976, and *The Experience of Inner Healing*, Waco: Word 1977; Michael Scanlon, *Inner Healing*, New York: Paulist 1974; on inner healing as related to confession particularly, see Michael Scanlon, *The Power in Penance*, Notre Dame: Ave Maria 1972.

## Chapter Two

1. See, for example, Claus Westermann, 'The Role of the Lament in the Theology of the Old Testament', *Interpretation* 28, 1974, 20-38, on which I depend in this chapter; see also his similar article (in various language editions) in number 9, 1976, of *Concilium*.

2. For example, see Psalms 22, 39, 42, 44, 51, (a cry for spiritual healing), 69, 74, 102, 130, 140, 142. Three psalms of lament for the nation are Psalms 60, 79 and 80.

3. The translation is a slight adaptation of Delbert Hiller's translation in the Anchor Bible Series: *Lamentations*, New York: Doubleday 1972, 96.
4. See Col. 3.16; Eph. 5.19.


## Chapter Three

1. For a theological reflection on Jesus' interior experience of his passion, see Gerald O'Collins, *The Calvary Christ*, London: SCM Press and Philadelphia: Westminster Press 1977. For a theological discussion of the meaning of the cross today, see R. Faricy, M. Flick and G. O'Collins, *The Cross Today*, New York: Paulist, 1978. For a spiritual theology of the cross in Jesus' life and in Christian life, see John Navone, *A Theology of Failure*, New York: Paulist 1974.
2. Nor does anything else; a mystery is precisely something we can learn more and more about, but never fully understand (*Baltimore Catechism*).
3. Leopold Sabourin, in *Sin, Redemption, and Sacrifice*, Rome: Biblical Institute Press 1970, 167; Sabourin has an extensive study of expiation, 120-289.
4. *The Prayers of Jesus in Their Contemporary Setting*, published by the Study Centre for Christian-Jewish Relations, London: 1977, 15-16.
5. I am following the careful and convincing exegesis of Ignace de la Potterie, in 'La sete di Gesù morente e l'interpretazione giovannea della sua morte in croce', *La sapienza della croce oggi*, Turin: Elle Di Ci 1976, vol. I, 33-49, who points out the need to read the phrase 'I thirst' in the light of the other references of John's gospel to thirst.
6. J. Terence Forestell, *The Word of the Cross*, Rome: Biblical Institute Press 1974: 'The primary symbolism of the water and the blood should probably be seen in the light of the same passage of Zechariah (13.1). In the context of the gospel the water from the side of Christ can only symbolize the gift of living water which he promised to the Samaritan woman and of which he declared himself the source at the feast of Tabernacles. The death of Christ releases the streams of eternal life for men' (p. 89). Besides Zechariah 13.1, clean and purifying

water that represents the Spirit of God in the New Covenant is referred to in Ezek. 36.25; cf. Psalm 51.2; Isa. 44.3.

7. Stanislaus Lyonnet, *Annotationes in priorem epistolam ad Corinthios* (class notes, Rome 1965-66), 44; quoted in S. Virgulin, 'La croce come potenza di Dio in I Cor. 1.18-24', *La sapienza della croce oggi*, vol. I, 15.

8. Dennis Hamm, 'To Heal as Jesus Healed?', unpublished paper written for and presented to an ecumenical conference, Roman Catholic and Assemblies of God, on divine healing, 15-16 April 1977, Springfield, Missouri, 4.

9. I have followed, with slight changes, John L. McKenzie's translation in the Anchor Bible: *Second Isaiah*, New York: Doubleday 1968, 129-30.

## Chapter Four

1. 'Sermo de redemptionis nostrae', *Opera omnia*, vol. IX, Rome: Ad claras aquas 1901, 264c and 265d.

2. New York: Macmillan 1969.

3. New York: Paulist 1978, 239.

4. I am grateful to Matthew and Dennis Linn for the basic idea of this chapter and the previous chapter: that Jesus, in approaching his death, went through the five stages of dying of Elizabeth Kübler-Ross; we talked about this as they were beginning to write *Healing Life's Hurts*.

5. See Matthew and Dennis Linn, *Healing Life's Hurts*, New York: Paulist 1978, 180-8.

6. *Healing Life's Hurts*, 236-7. The Linns also give valuable advice on how to pray for healing of fear and anxiety about the future by meditating on Jesus' agony in the garden (237-8), and on praying to forgive as Jesus forgives by meditating on his seven last words from the cross (231-5).

7. The fourteen stations are: 1. Jesus is condemned to death; 2. Jesus receives the cross; 3. Jesus falls the first time; 4. Jesus meets his mother; 5. Simon of Cyrene takes the cross; 6. Veronica wipes the face of Jesus; 7. Jesus falls a second time; 8. the women of Jerusalem weep for Jesus; 9. Jesus falls a third time; 10. Jesus is stripped of his garments; 11. the crucifiction; 12. Jesus dies; 13. Jesus is taken down from the cross; 14. Jesus is buried.

For that matter, it is not necessary to stick to the number fourteen; in the beginning of the practice of the stations, from the early thirteenth century until the strong Franciscan preaching of the fourteen stations in the eighteenth century, we find anywhere from six to fifteen stations. For example, the early seventeenth-century Jesuits preached seven: Gethsemane, the house of Annas, the house of Caiaphas, Pilate's quarters, Herod's palace, Pilate's quarters a second time, Mount Calvary (see the *Dictionnaire de spiritualité*, vol. II, col. 2587); the seven stations have the advantage of being rigorously biblical.

8. *Le lettere di Santa Caterina da Siena*, ed. P. Misciattelli, Florence: Mazocco 1939, 36.

9. *The Revelations of Divine Love*, chapter 24; in the Penguin edition, 170; in James Walsh's translation, London: Burns and Oates, 1961, 87.

10. *The Spiritual Exercises of St. Ignatius*, trans. L. Puhl, Westminster, Md: Newman 1967.

11. Ibid., no. 53.

12. Ibid., no. 193.

13. Ibid., no. 203.

14. Ibid., no. 206.

15. Ibid.

16. Ibid., 'Third Week' *passim*.

17. Stephen Sundborg, 'Ignatian Spirituality of the Cross' unpublished paper, 3.

18. Ibid.

19. *Exercises*, nos. 297 and 298.

20. This kind of prayer seems especially indicated where the hurts to be healed involve women – for example, a poor relationship with one's mother or sister or aunt, or a fear of women; also, for the healing of resentment against authority.

This is traditional Christian practice, to pray to Jesus for healing through the intercession of his mother. About 560, Romanos the Hymn Composer, as the antiphon verse of his hymn 'The Leper', has this prayer for inner healing to Jesus Christ: 'Just as you cleansed the leper of his sickness, all-powerful One, by your mercy heal what is wrong with our souls, through the intervention on our behalf of the Mother of God, O you doctor of our souls . . .': *Romanos le Mélode*, *hymnes*, Introduction, critical text, translation and notes by J. Grosdidier de Matons, vol. II, Sources chrétiennes no. 110, Paris: Cerf 1965, 360.

21. As does the eighth-century Irish poet, Blathmac: 'Come to me, loving Mary, that I may keen (lament) with you your very dear one.' What follows is a long poem of lament with Mary. Donal Flanigan, 'Mary in the Poems of Blathmac', in *De cultu mariano saeculis VI-XI*, vol. III, Rome: Pontificia academis mariana internationalis 1972, 269.

22. Prayer from the English Missal, memorial of Our Lady of Ransom, September 24.

## *Chapter Five*

1. Peter Hocken, *You He Made Alive*, London: Darton, Longman, and Todd 1974, 79.

2. *Dogmatic Constitution on the Catholic Faith*, *Dei Filius*, canon 5 of chapter I.

3. *Ecrits spirituels*, ed. R. P. Philipon, Paris: Seuil 1974, 203-4.

4. 5.25-26; 7.16; 13.13; 17.15-18; 18.43; 19.37-38; 23.47; 24.53.

5. See also 14.1-5; 15.3-4; 19.1-8.

6. Commentary on Psalm 102, *Corpus christianorum, series latina*, vol. 40, *Ennarrationes in psalmos CI-CL*, Turnholt: Brepols 1956, 1453.

7. Commentary on Psalm 134, ibid., 1937.

8. The already classic theological study of the gift of tongues is: Francis A. Sullivan, 'Speaking in Tongues', *Lumen Vitae* 31, 1976, 145-70. See also his excellent brief treatment of the gift of tongues, 'Langues (don de)', in the *Dictionnaire de spiritualité*, vol. IX, Paris: Beauchesne 1975, cols. 223-6; there is appended a useful interdisciplinary bibliography.

9. Op. cit., 83 and 82.

10. *Tongue Speaking*, London: Hodder and Stoughton 1973, 220-2. Virginia Hine, looking at speaking in tongues scientifically and in the light of other scientific studies, concludes: 'Through a functional approach to the phenomenon, we have come to assess glossalalia [speaking in tongues] as a non-pathological linguistic behaviour which functions in the context of the Pentecostal movement as one component in the generation of commitment. As such, it operates in social

change . . . and in personal change, providing powerful motivation for attitudinal and behavioral changes in the direction of group ideals.' ('Pentecostal Glossolalia: Toward a Functional Interpretation', *Journal for the Scientific Study of Religion* 7, 1969, 225).

11. H. Muhlen, 'The Person of the Holy Spirit', in *The Holy Spirit and Power*, ed. K. McDonnell, New York: Doubleday 1975, 27.

12. Thomas Aquinas, *Summa Theologiae*, III, q. 8, a. 1 ad 3; III *Sent.*, d. 13, q. 2, a. 2, sol. 2.

13. Thomas Aquinas, I *Sent.*, d. 15, q. 1, a. 1 ad 1; d. 17, q. 1, a. 1; d. 30, q. 1, a. 3.

14. John 14.16; 14.26; 15.26; 16.7; cf. I John 2.1.

15. John 14.25-26; 16.12-23; 15.26-27. See H. Benjamin, 'Pneuma in John and Paul', *Biblical Theology Bulletin* 5, 1975, 27-48.

16. I Cor. 12.28-30; 13.1-3; 14.6; 14.26; Rom. 12.6-8; Eph. 4.11.

17. Section 23.

## Chapter Six

1. For a recent study of Jesus' Lordship in the New Testament, see; David M. Hay, *Glory at the Right Hand: Psalm 110 in Early Christianity*, SBL Monograph Series XVIII, Nashville New York 1973.

2. In the New Testament, Psalm 110 is most often referred to in terms of Jesus' sitting at the right hand of the Father, and so as an interpretation of the resurrection and the ascension. And it is used as a messianic text, frequently in conjunction with the word 'Christ' (the anointed Messiah). So, although it is at the origin of the idea that Jesus is Lord, its use in the primitive church was chiefly functional, to explain what happened to Jesus as the Messiah in his resurrection and ascension: he was exalted, made Lord, given dominion, and sits at the right hand of the Father. However, it was used at the same time to express Jesus' Lordship, or dominion; it is sometimes used together with Psalm 8.6 (in Eph. 1.21-22; I Cor. 15.25, 27; Heb. 2.6-8).

3. Number 10.